ETHNIC IDENTITY AND NATIONAL INTEGRATION

ABOUT THE EDITOR

The Editor, a Fulbright scholar and Ph.D. in Government from Cornell University, New York, is a senior academic with a number of publications to his credit. His earlier works on urban government and politics, political development, population and education are of seminal importance. A former Vice-Chancellor of Jamia Millia Islamia, he is currently the Director of Gandhian Institute of Studies, Rajghat, Varanasi.

ETHNIC IDENTITY AND NATIONAL INTEGRATION

Edited by
ALI ASHRAF
Director
Gandhian Institute of Studies
Varanasi

CONCEPT PUBLISHING COMPANY, NEW DELHI 110059

ISBN 81-7022-502-7

First Published 1994

Published and Printed by
Ashok Kumar Mittal
Concept Publishing Company
A/15-16, Commercial Block, Mohan Garden
NEW DELHI 110059 (India)

Lasertypeset by
Printing Express
H-13, Bali Nagar
NEW DELHI 110015

PREFACE

1991 was the year when the USSR was declared dead. The momentous event of the century marked, first the collapse of a massive communist regime and, secondly the break-up of a vast multi-ethnic State. That a bizarre phenomenon like the Soviet Union would not last for long and eventually yield under the weight of its bureaucratic and political regimentation and back-breaking cost of security and system maintenance was expected. No one, however, hoped or feared the abrupt and sudden fall of the giant.

It was under the shadow of the events taking place in the Soviet Union and East Europe that a Seminar was organised at the Gandhian Institute of Studies, Varanasi. A large number of participants attended and a good deal of discussion took place. Some of the distinguished participants like Dr. Vibhuti Narain Singh, Chancellor, Banaras Hindu University, the late Prof. Raja Ram Shastri, Prof. Amlan Dutta, and Prof. Chetkar Jha enriched the deliberations by oral contributions which are not included in the book in the form of chapters. Their wise words nevertheless guided and informed the discussions and set a tone which is reflected in the Introduction and Conclusion. However, the responsibility for these rests entirely with the Editor.

A seminar is nothing if it is not provocative enough to produce sharp interaction and a clash of perspectives. To create intellectual integration out of individual divergences is on a smaller scale as difficult and important as the achievement of political integration out of ethnic diversity. As in the nation-building activity so in intellectual exercise our beacon light is Mahatma Gandhi. We are guided in our intellectual pursuits as in our public views by what we consider important and useful for our people and country. There are both internal and external aspects of life: the internal is the moral and the external is the environmental. The internal or moral force must guide the environmental and political activities. India has a great reserve of latent moral force, but it is overshadowed by the manifest political humdrum. The future of India depends on our political response to our problems. So long India has survived in spite of its political *Shenanigans* but it requires a firm and committed political leadership to maintain a steady course of national integration and development.

I am grateful to the participants and my colleagues at the Gandhian Institute of Studies for their contribution to the success of the Seminar. I am also indebted to Miss Lata Srivastava who read the papers and helped in preparing the script and format of the contents of this book. I would like to acknowledge the secretarial assistance provided by Mr. John Mathew and Mahendra Prasad of my office at the Gandhian Institute. I would also like to acknowledge the debt I owe to the Publishers.

March 1993 ALI ASHRAF
Varanasi

CONTENTS

LIST OF CONTRIBUTORS

Prof. Ali Ashraf
Director
Gandhian Institute of Studies
Rajghat,
VARANASI-221001.

Prof. Anirudha Gupta
Department of African Studies
Jawaharlal Nehru University
NEW DELHI

Dr. Chandrakala Padia
Department of Political Science
Banaras Hindu University
VARANASI-221005

Dr. Sachchidananda
Formerly Director
A.N. Sinha Institute of Social Studies
PATNA

Prof. L.N. Sharma
Professor of Political Science
(Presently) Senior Fellow Indian Council of Social Science Research
NEW DELHI

Shri Mohd. Showeb
Lecturer
Gandhian Institute of Studies
Rajghat, VARANASI-221001

Prof. M.G. Husain
Department of Psychology
Jamia Millia Islamia
Jamia Nagar
NEW DELHI-110025.

Dr. Sushma Suri
Department of Psychology
Jamia Millia Islamia
Jamia Nagar
NEW DELHI-110025

Dr. Peter Ronald D'Souza
Department of Political Science
University of Goa
GOA.

Prof. Mahendra Prasad Singh
Department of Political Science
University of Delhi
DELHI-110007

Prof. S.M. Dubey
Department of Sociology
Dibrugarh University
DIBRUGARH

Dr. Vijay Ranjan Dutta
Reader in Political Science
Gandhian Institute of Studies
Rajghat, VARANASI-221001

Dr. M. Aram
President
Shanti Ashram
COIMBATORE-641042.

Prof. Ramjee Singh
Chairperson
Department of Gandhian Thought
University of Bhagalpur
BHAGALPUR

John Rex
Professor Emeritus
Centre for Research in Ethnic Relations
University of Warwick.

1

INTRODUCTION

ALI ASHRAF

Discussion of political issues in the Third World has suffered due to several internal and external reasons. The Third World has been characterized by a tradition of religious obscurantism where words have been taken as immutable and unalterable; and it lacks social philosophy based on a discourse and discussion to establish standards of judgement and facts of truth and relevance. And whatever philosophical legacy exists is more in the nature of theological expositions rather than critical analysis of concepts and methods. The persistence of classical languages as the repository of philosophy and religion indeed closes the door to understanding and reduces knowledge from a dynamic process to a mass of doctrinaire pedantry. The emancipation and improvement of intellectual discourse has been accordingly hampered by the bondage to the authority of books in classical languages of antiquity or alien languages of modern masters. The development of a vigorous literature of social philosophy remains arrested by the fact that vernacular languages are squeezed between the theological literature of the past and the imitative framework borrowed from the West. We are, therefore, unable to discuss our problems in the spirit of sincerity, simplicity and integrity.

A serious problem arises because the social framework of conceptualization, analysis and identification of the problems or issues is set by the West. It is important to note that in spite of social and political pluralism of the Western countries, Britain, France, the USA and Germany, the intellectual tradition and the political domain are finely woven together, each drawing upon the other, correcting and improving each other. The universities are very much part of the political as well as cultural complex of the country. The role of Harvard or Oxford in moulding the mind and contributing to the political and cultural leadership is too obvious and well known to be ignored. The Church and the State may be separate in the secular West, but the universities and other intellectual centres have taken the place of the Church as a source of intellectual and moral inputs in the political process. The universities have indeed become the secular and intellectual equivalent of the Church in relation to the State. And they are not two separate streams but very well integrated and inter-twined in the mainstream of culture and politics. The only difference is that the universities are becoming more and more multiversities and, therefore, allow for greater independence of thought, and yet within the common framework of their civilization.

Based on such intellectual resilience and vigour, and aided by the advancement in information technology and vast resources, the West has managed to achieve a dominant status and a unity of civilization that is unrivalled. The Western intellectuals and professionals have opportunities to travel and enjoy access to sources of information not available to the Third World scholars. The whole world is a field as well as an arena for the Western scholarship and statesmanship. Political issues are after all not just social problems, but the problems that are highlighted, articulated and moralized as agenda for political action. Contemporary political phenomena are indeed artefacts or constructs that are formed and lifted out of the raw field and held as issues to suit the academic interests of Western scholars or the global strategic interests of the Western society. The Third World has nothing comparable to cultivate. Ethnicity, for example, like modernity is a theme raised and discussed by the Western scholars to create dichotomies where it is only an aspect of life and part of a long civilization. Change and continuity, conflict and reconciliation, separation and integration are characteristics of all societies, more or less; and these must be understood within the parameters of culture and history of a people. But these phenomena in the Third World are presented as if these are problems unique and specific signs of the backward South.

II

The recent developments in the former Soviet Union and East Europe have become the point of departure for all economic and political discussions. The economic change and the issues of socialism or liberalism, of regulation and privatization are peripheral to this study, but the collapse of the Union of Soviet Socialist Republics is of central importance. the break-up of the USSR has coincided with the demise of communism; it has indeed shaken confidence in the political unions of disparate and discordant units such as the USSR was. However, the very fact that the USSR was a union of disparate and discordant units raises a number of questions. First, the union of Baltic States was effected under circumstances of compulsion and not even universally recognized as legal or legitimate. Secondly, the occupation of Central Asian republics predated the Soviet revolution and was an act of imperial expansion under the Czars. Thirdly, the regime of one party regimentation and the stranglehold of centralized planning with all the emphasis on defence and heavy industries allowed little autonomy and opportunity to the republics to carve out their destiny in a free and productive manner. There is no doubt that the Soviet demise raises serious questions about the proper and productive organization of political economy in terms of its effects for economic development and political stability of pluralist societies. These questions call for reinterpretation and reorganization of several urgent political issues before new nations seeking to establish their political unity in the midst of their divisive elements.

Socio-economic development and national integration have been the two basic objectives of India's political development since Independence. The national consensus about these issues – now often derisively called the Nehruvian model – upholds socialism, secularism and democracy as the foundation of India's escape from poverty and disunity. The recent innovations in the industrial and trade policy heralds liberalization but not reversal in the economic objectives, for India has followed the policy of mixed economy and not full-blooded centralized planning and regimentation. The evils of regulation, of permit and licence *raj*, and the misuse and mal-functioning of public enterprises have been distortions compounded by the growing empowerment and expansion of bureaucracy and political corruption. The need to encourage private enterprise and free it from the unnecessary controls of administration has been felt in the past also, but little concrete was done due to expediency and opportunism. Anyway the point that needs to be made here is the fact that the Nehruvian model is not like the Soviet model in terms of economic controls and political regime; and poverty alleviation, employment generation and social security, health and educational opportunities for more and more people, remain as valid today as in the early days of India's Independence. The change in the economic policy is more of tactical than strategic nature to avoid wasteful expenditure and inefficient and non-productive policies and programmes rather than to modify the social objectives of employment, social security, and equal opportunity for all.

The problem of ethnicity and national unity is the other national goal that requires management with understanding and vision. India is proverbial for its diversity – diversity of races, religions and languages. The cause of unity in the midst of diversity was dear to the freedom fighters and continues to be a primary and vital commitment. The cause has become an issue since the recent demands for state autonomy and, in the cases of Punjab and Kashmir or Assam, even of separation. The states reorganization on the basis of linguistic-regional considerations even before the end of the first decade of Independence was a concession to the linguistic diversity of the country. The linguistic reorganization of states accentuated and made permanent the *regional* factor in the Indian State. Language and culture formed the basis of regionalism and through the four decades of freedom, the tendency towards regional identity and assertion has grown. The three-language formulae also has not been implemented in the right spirit in all states and the dilemma between the alien and elitist English and the native but synthetic Hindi continues to cause stalemate in the development of a national language and political culture. The regional language and culture buttressed by State administration and education have made regionalism of greater importance underlying the demand for economic and political autonomy. India seems to grow more in its regional identities than in its national identity. Hence the growing tensions between a Centre equipped with enormous military, police and bureaucratic power and constituent States threatened with the erosion of their autonomy and opportunity for participation in national and regional development.

A question being asked is whether regional identity makes the Union of India and the Indian State fragile and vulnerable to forces of disintegration. What is the nature and magnitude of the threat arising from regionalism? And what are the best ways of fostering and maintaining the unity of India? These are serious and important questions that require a fresh look, free from the hangover of pre-partition communal perspectives. Some people have also raised the question whether India would have been partitioned if it were not for the Muslims. Religion was undoubtedly a predominant factor in the partition of India, but it would be very myopic to analyse the contemporary problems of Indian unity in religious terms. It needs to be understood that the problems of Kashmir and Punjab are also not just religious –

they are the extreme forms of regionalism reinforced by religious fundamentalism. Unless a religion is also a regional phenomenon, it cannot become a force of secession. And plenty of contemporary turmoil in India emanates from other social divisions like caste and tribe as well as regional and religious factors. Besides the question of causes and conditions of turmoil, the nature of political response to these problems is of utmost importance. The problem of India's unity arises not only because of the divisive forces of region and religion, and sociological factors such as caste and tribe but above all due to the political weaknesses and mistakes especially of the Centre. It may be argued that the political factor is the most crucial and decisive in maintaining or disrupting a balance between the forces of regional identity and national integration.

Except for the tribal societies, very few political units are so fully homogeneous and cohesive that they can maintain unity without effort and struggle and organization. Even the tiny City States of antiquity were ridden with differences and conflicts. It is the task of statesmanship to build Nation and State out of discordant and disparate elements. Unity may, of course, be created by conquest and compulsion but history shows that such unity seldom endures and the cost of such unity is high in terms of life and culture. This is the stark and in a way happy lesson to be learnt from the disintegration of the Soviet Union. In this age of electronic media and mass communication it has become difficult more than ever to hold large segments of dissatisfied and divergent elements within the yoke of dictatorship for long.

The danger, on the other hand, comes from inability to define the limits of autonomy and stop short of secession and disintegration. Striking a balance between regional autonomy and national unity, between the rights of groups and the demands of a common framework is the essence of the political process which to succeed must be a dynamic process of negotiation and reconciliation, especially in the case of India which, with all its regional, ethnic and social diversity, has the foundation of a democratic constitution and a composite culture. Unless we dissipate the abiding and deep-rooted assets of a long civilization characterized by social pluralism and reconciliation, the infrastructure of a military and administrative system and the legal framework of a federal constitution, the challenge to our national integration is not unmanageable.

The cause of national unity and integration would be better served if we recognize and nourish the environment of socio-cultural and political pluralism. Any attempt to curtail such pluralism would be fraught with avoidable violence and inevitable failure. The two political expressions of this pluralism are federation and democracy. In spite of state powers, a federation tends to create its own unity by strengthening the Centre. Through control of the military and civil authorities, higher economic levers, transport and foreign relations including trade, the Centre wields authority unrivalled by any power possessed by the constituent States. So long as it commands the levers of unity, the Centre can afford to allow ample decentralization of authority not only to the State but also through the States to local institutions of grassroot democracy. There has been some debate in recent times about Article 370, but nothing could be more short-sighted than to indulge in sensational and counter-productive measures in the spirit of pseudopatriotism which, without vision and wisdom, is liable to degenerate into national tribalism.

Along with federalism, democracy is necessary. We have a framework of political democracy, but it is also tarnished by violence and irresponsibility. Elections are not enough to make a democracy; and we cannot claim that our elections are free and fair. At best they are a farce, and at worst subversive, ridden as they are with social and legal violence. The success of democracy would require many things but, above all, decentralization and participation of people in the management of their affairs; the political accountability of the people's representatives for public interests, and not just to their constituencies of castes and communities; and a commitment to social equality and justice for all the citizens. It is unfortunate and very sad indeed that all these three conditions are conspicuous in India by their absence. The blessings of India's pluralism and federation are very largely nullified by the absence of decentralization, political responsibility and social equality. The cause of national unity and political stability suffers on account of the mounting frustrations and tensions arising from social inequality, political irresponsibility and administrative authoritarianism. The political parties in or out of power find scapegoats in the "divisive" forces and do precious little to improve the political and administrative performance to solve the problems of the people. To cover up their own defects and failures they attempt to achieve integration by hook or by crook. The diversionary tactics tend to exacerbate rather than mitigate the forces of separatism or disunity. The weakness of the regime emanates indeed more from its political distortions than from its ecological diversities.

III

Today the nation-state faces a challenge all over the world, and the immediate reflex seems to be to divide and sub-divide on the ethnic line. Nationalism and ethnic subnatonalism in many States are locked in a mortal combat between integration and secession. The nationality problem with its slogan of national self-determination is reappearing in the garb of ethnic assertiveness. There are some significant differences though technology, economy and environment issues have modified the world in respect of its common concern of the survival and sustainable development of the earth and humanity. The world is also weary of war and nuclear arms. The irony of the situation, however, is that there are contradictory trends towards globalism and regional cooperation on the one hand and ethnic separatism on the other. But paradoxes also have their explanations.

What is the naturc of separate ethnic claims? One view is that they are the results of psychological and cultural self-view based on distinct language, religion, script and historical traditions of the masses. Therefore, ethnic passions, ideologies, movements and parties are all an outcome of elemental drives at popular level. The masses are naturally inclined to ethnicized politics and, therefore, all communal activities only represent the masses. All the above gathers around a civilizational viewpoint of ethnicity – that ethnic discord and ethnic solidarity are rooted in convergence of divergence of civilizational identity. Marx Webber says that the cultural classes, i.e. the *literatti* and those who are deeply concerned with the question of status, were also the ones who were the most passionate in their religious espousals. That brings us to the other view of the nature of ethnic assertions which says that they are not assertions from below based on any real differences. They are essentially *ideationalization* of some differences by a certain class and they are not the natural ways in which the masses behave. Manifestations of ethnicity in *Inchain* Politics take root at the top and are broadcast below. That means ethnicized politics is "conspiratorial in Nature", inasmuch as it is fashioned in a deliberate and calculated manner. But even these *ideationalizations* of ethnic differences do not hold the imagination of the masses always and everywhere. The study of occasions and locations of successful ideationalization of ethnic differences is in place to understand the nature of ethnicity.*

---

* Marx Webber in *Economy and Society*, Guenther Roth and Claus Witlich (eds.), N.Y. : Bedminister Press, 1968.

Anyway more dangerous and still underemphasized aspect is the psychological aspect. Even if all ethnic eruptions happen to be basically conspiratorial and seemingly dirty devices of group mobilization of political and economic issues, there is no denying the fact that each ethnic outburst is stored in the collective memory and slowly but surely proceeds to contribute in the crystallization of individual identity which is basically insecure, bigotted and ethnicized in a wrong sense. This ethnicization does not have a rational basis of group mobilization and is increasingly destructive and at times self-consuming. The growing enormity of destruction of life and property, the venom and violence evidenced during more recent ethnic violence in India and abroad is testimony to the fact that ethnicized psyche is a more basic threat to national integration than the ethnicized politics. Ethnic politics after all might be democratic and peaceful; but ethnic psyche is prone to violence and destruction.

As a result of the failure of secular democratic politics and aggressive ethnicity two possibilities emerge. First, religious fundamentalism could overtake the entire Indian sub-continent. Which means that all relevant aspects of secular life are imbued with religious sanction. Thus, religious and communal passions could be aroused to eliminate or smother ethnic or cultural pluralism in order to create political unity. The second possibility could be the emergence of secular totalitarianism under a dictatorship to ward off ethnic or regional separatism. Both the possibilities are inimical to democracy, autonomy of social and ethnic groups and peace in the region. Totalitarian States based on either religious fundamentalism or national chauvinism would negate the basis of internal democracy and regional cooperation. The answer to the question of ethnic or regional identity and national unity of India is a genuine federal democracy – and more of it rather than less. Commitment to the national cause and confidence in the peoples of diverse identities as well as one's own would go a long way to reconcile regional or cultural identity with national integration than any measure of false patriotism. Is it not possible to broaden the base of political system? Why should National Integration only mean more use of State force? Why should it not mean a conscious effort to share power nearer to the ground? It is relevant here to quote Lord Acton:

> If we take the establishment of liberty for the realisation of duties to be the end of civil society, we must conclude that those states are substantially more perfect which . . . include various distinct nationalities without oppressing them. Those in which no mixture

of races has occurred are imperfect; and those in which its efforts have disappeared are decrepit. A state which is incompetent to satisfy different races condemns itself; a state which labours to neutralise, to absorb or to expel them, destroys its own vitality; a state which does not include them is destitute of the chief basis of self-government.*

IV

Contributions to the present volume focus on the question of ethnicity and its repercussions on National Integration.

Anirudha Gupta in his paper shows that ethnicity as a historical and political pattern of identity formation in the Third World society cannot be wished away. Use of force to maintain the integrity of a Nation State only gives rise to the centrifugal pulls. He recommends the rejection of the concept of Nation State and adoption of an approach where ethnicity has a large role to play.

Ms. Chandrakala Padia's paper puts forth a critique of the arguments of D.L. Sheth and Ashish Nandy questioning the relevance of Nation State model in representing its people and asking for a search for some other kind of political arrangement to "contain the forces of ethnicity". Ms. Padia on her part says that Nation State is a model which can adjust itself to the individual character and major interests of different ethnic groups. There was the possibility of enlightened individuals of ethnic groups coming forward to contain the anti-democratic forces of ethnicity. She sees the role of education in moulding the ethnic ways of life to promote the cause of national integration.

Prof. Sachchidananda attempts a precise definition of ethnicity and maintains that ethnicity is a challenge to major paradigms of development. He argues that some aspects of ethnicity appear to be disruptive and offered to national integration. This however need not be so if the potential of ethnic identities is mobilized in a thoughtful and constructive manner, especially by according a measure of recognition and autonomy for all the nationalities and ethnic groups. His conclusion is that there can be no integration without participation by all groups in the determination of national policies.

L.N. Sharma's paper, "Ethnic Identity and National Integration in

---

* Quoted in *India Divided* by Rajendra Prasad, "National and Multinational", p. 29.

India", recounts the history of various ethnic groups coming to India and getting assimilated into its life. He says that the assimilative capacity of society received a negative jerk during the Muslim period as the two ethnic groups, namely, Hindus and Muslims, faced each other in the background of completely different situations. This was followed by the British period when the policy of "Divide and Rule" followed by the government further acted to sharpen the ethnic division. While there is nothing wrong in maintaining cultural pluralism, there is need to "tone down" the ethnic conflicts. This could be achieved if there are strong social movements to prevent the aggregation of ethnic identities out of proportion, as well as governmental effort to create an equitable economic development in all regions and among all communities.

Mohd. Showeb in his paper "Identity of Indian Muslims and Problems of National Integration" stresses the fact that the Muslim community has a very differentiated identity from linguistic, cultural, economic and social points of view. He underlines the fact that the Muslim community is closer to other cohabiting groups in terms of language, cultural moorings and social stratification and is economically as differentiated as others. Any exploration of the process of national integration must take this into account in understanding the fact of local, regional or cultural identity and the process of integration.

M.G. Husain and Sushma Suri in their paper, "Ethnicity, Indian National Identity and National Integration", say that national identity was not opposed to ethnic identity, unless and until Majoritarian State threatens to destroy pluralism, and force assimilation. As a matter of sociological fact, identity formation is the product of dialectics between individual and society, and of the membership of the individual in the social groups and the real or perceived satisfaction of the individual from the membership of the same. The social groups to which minorities belong and the ascribed inferiority of the minorities along with a 'Closed' identity reinforced by real or perceived deprivation together may account for their having a weak national feeling and strong ethnic identity.

Sushma Suri and M.G. Husain in their joint paper, "Deprived and Non-Deprived Ethnic Groups – A Study of Their Identity", try to unfold the psychological aspects of identity formation through an empirical survey. Their findings suggest that there is a correlation between the strong ethnic identity and level of deprivation – which most of the minority groups suffer from. The ethnic groups face each other as deprived and non-deprived groups. Being in conflict with non-deprived groups breeds a stronger ethnic identity. And a stronger ethnic identity breeds further conflicts, and it goes on and on as a cycle. Under such circumstances the option to have a separate group identity keeps them stuck to the deprived group only. These groups, therefore, must endeavour to have a not too distinct at the same time not too diffuse identity.

Peter Ronald D'Souza stresses that integration is not a descriptive but a value-loaded concept. But in spite of the fact that it did not necessarily carry universally commendatory responses there are certain objective interests around which all communities can be brought together on the basis of subjective understanding of the same. Therefore, the protagonists of democracy should not shy away from activization of latent identities and competition to defend one's interest as they are merely conflicts resulting from imposition of an institutional design of equality over those based on unequality and the asymmetrical power structure of this country.

Notwithstanding these problems, equality, participation, competitive defence of interests, etc., should be encouraged to foster democracy.

Prof. M.P. Singh in his paper, "To Govern or Not to Govern? The Dilemma of the New Party System", talks about the role of party system in a political system where consensus has broken down. Party system as an instrument of "interent aggregation" is an important mechanism which links together the civil society on the one hand and the political system on the other. But the shape of the Indian party system has been changing and these are not the days of "One Party Dominant System", various identities whether religio-communal or otherwise have started pulling apart. In such a situation numerous identities have taken to streets – while the role of political institutions and constitutional authorities tends to be marginalized. The coalition phase in being taken only as a phase enpassant and the political party seems to be in the wishful wait for the return of the same old "One Party Dominant System" in order to rise up to the task of governance. But given the fact and need of modernization and industrialization the polity is going to be further differentiated and specialized in structure and function. Independence of various pressure groups from the hegemony of various political parties serves as an evidence. He then points to the pleas Prof. Rajni Kothari has been making for a "new solidarity where the various diversities found meaning". He sees the urgency to carry out the institutional reforms that Prof. Kothari and the Sarkaria Commission suggest to bring this about.

Prof. S.M. Dubey in his paper,"Ethnic Identity and National Integration – Meaning, Concept and Issues", deals with the meaning, concept and issues of integration and ethnic identity from a structural-functional point of view. He accounts for the forces of national integration and ethnicity in the twin processes of "boundary formation and maintenance" in a system, which take place almost simultaneously. A balance between them is achieved through education, urbanization, industrialization, technological advancement, physical, occupational and social mobility and also mass media. But in India these stabilizing factors have failed.

Dr. V.R. Dutta puts forth the Gandhian perspective through this paper, "Ethnicity and National Integration – A Gandhian Perspective". He says that the assertion of divergent identities and national integration cannot be reconciled either through linguistic solutions or centralization of the polity or by adopting a Western developmental model. He feels that only the establishment of "little democracies" of the district level, use of symbols of national integration, a political culture assuring the dignity of individual and starting of a series of dialogues to resolve various issues could help national integration.

Dr. M. Aram in his paper, "Participation: A Key to Integration", takes the Naga case. He very incisively describes how the identity formation took place among the hitherto scattered Naga tribes and their resultant suspicion of the Indian mainstream. He goes on to recount various efforts, especially those of Jaiparakash Narayan's, to start a parliamentary process among the Naga people which was ultimately capped with success. But, he says, the situation is quite far from a happy one on the national level. The effort which was made to spur the Nagas into participation in order to ensure their integration into the Nation is no longer being made in similar situations today in other parts of the country. The political system is not federal enough, the developmental process is not participatory enough, and the education system lacks the quality to bring about participation of various identities to ensure integration. He agrees to the regional model of identity and integration in the international politics through SAARC just on the model of the EEC. This is the demand of today's changing world.

. The paper of Prof. Ramjee Singh entitled "Ramjanambhoomi-Babri Masjid Controversy: A Non-governmental Solution" deals with the ticklish controversy surrounding Ayodhya mandir-masjid issue. The paper has been overtaken by the events culminating in the demolition of the disputed structure, but since there is fresh controversy about the construction of a temple and the mosque, there is persistent stalemate clouding the atmosphere of the country. Hence the suggestion of Prof. Ramjee Singh regarding the desirability of arbitration is still of value in resolving the lingering conflict. The importance of Prof. Singh's argument lies in the possibility of a non-governmental resolution of conflict through goodwill and wisdom in order to avoid violence and tensions among the religious communities of India, and establish what the author calls the culture of compassion.

John Rex in his paper, "Political Sociology of a Multi-Cultural Society", tries to bring forth difficulties in the "two domain" theory like Honyford had proposed. This theory sought to present an alternative to national integration during the late eighties. The theory talked about the co-existence of Public Domain –based on equality of opportunity and shared political culture and the Private Domain based on cultural diversities. Prof. John Rex points out the practical difficulties in keeping both the domains from spilling into each other, and subsequent problems.

The value of these papers exceeds their content and lies in the discussions they generated over three days of the Seminar. The omission of much of the deliberations is an omission but it is hoped that the papers do present a unified impression; but it is difficult to capture in print the integration of common framework evolving out of differences of views. One hopes that these papers would make a useful contribution to the understanding of the problems of Ethnic Identity and National Integration.

2

ETHNIC CONFLICT:
Root of the Problem

ANIRUDHA GUPTA

At an international seminar on South Africa held in New Delhi (February 19-21, 1991), delegates from South Africa forcefully argued that the tribal warfares between Xhoxsa- and Zulu-speaking people were purely transitional. Such warfares, they argued, were deliberately fanned by the apartheid regime. Therefore, once the racist white power falls, Zulu-Xhoxsa relations will return to normal. They would all share a sense of belonging to an independent, non-racial and democratic South Africa.

They may have a valid point; and judging from their current preoccupation with a changing South Africa, it is natural for them to stress black unity more than any other aspect which could undermine the anti-apartheid cause. Their optimism is as fair or ebullient as the ones upheld by the nationalists all over Africa a decade or so ago. But, unfortunately, such enthusiasm did not last long. One by one, independent African countries were overtaken by internecine conflicts–tribal, regional or linguistic and racial – and the post-independent structures, carefully raised by the nationalists, fell like a house of cards. The debris, alas, only reminded one of the "fallacies of hope".[1] Thus, even as the strongly entrenched CPP of Ghana, asserted itself under Kwame Nkrumah, the relationship between the CPP and the Akan-speaking people of the north worsened. Any attempt at ethnic assertion by Akan and other minority groups was met by brutal force. The centralizing tendencies of the State made it an oppressive machine. No wonder that the civilians were pushed out by the soldiers–who held sway in one or other capacity ever since.

In Nigeria, the process was different. Unlike the CPP, there was no single party in Nigeria having support in three important regions–North (Hausa-speaking), West (Yaruba) and East (Ibo). The imbalance between the regions — not so much among rival tribes–led to a three-year civil war between what came to be called Biafra and the federal government. The result, again, was massive use of brutal force by the centre, collapse of civilian regime and rise of the military to power.

In Sudan, Chad and Ethiopia, conflicts were rooted in either racial differences or deep-rooted grievances of ethnic nationalities. The war between Nilotic south and Arabized north in Sudan has gone on endlessly–without securing peace or victory for either. Intra-tribal war in Chad led to several foreign interventions and, inevitably, widespread chaos and destruction. What about Ethiopia? Eritreans have all the attributes of a common heritage, language and territory, to merit the status of a separate nationality. Yet, self-determination of any type has been denied to them by both *ancien* and military regimes in Addis Ababa. Taking advantage of their struggle for self-determination, Somalis too sought to extend their sway across the Ethiopian borders.

It is a fact that ethnic and separatist movements were often exploited by outside powers–France in Biafra, Belgium in the Katanga, South Africa in the Angolan civil war and so on. But, over the three decades since most African countries had gained independence, two tendencies seem to have increasingly gained strength: *first,* determination of the ruling elite, mostly centred in the national capital, to maintain the country's unity at any cost. This has resulted in over-centralization of effective powers at the Centre and increasing marginalization of the peripheral regions. *Second*, an equally strong determination on the part of the minority communities or groups to gain autonomy or larger share of power to run their own affairs without undue interference from the Centre.

These two tendencies are not complementary; in fact, if anything, they are directly opposite. To keep the nation-state intact, the Centre uses power, more power, and finally brute force to suppress ethnic minorities. The process produces counter-use of force by the latter. In some sense, national politics gets permanently embroiled in violence, either political or military or both. How does one get release from this vicious–and self-destructive cycle.

The Africans have not still applied their minds to analyse the roots of ethnic conflict in order to reach at least a framework for remedial solutions. Nor have we, in India, either. In the whole of South Asia as in Africa, the integrity of the nation-state as handed over by the departing colonial powers remains the first and last doctrine in politics. It does not matter if a segment of the national population spills over into an adjoining territory–and, therefore, on its part tries to develop dual loyalty to the nation-state as well as to ethnic solidarity crossing over national boundaries. From the point of view of the Centre, this is subversive. The Ewas on the Ghana-Togo border live in both territories. In Togo, they constitute a majority and, therefore, their ties across the borders are not unwelcome. But, for the same reason, the Ewas, who are a minority in Ghana, are considered subversive in Ghana.

The situation in South Asia is not very different : the Tamils in Sri Lanka have intimate historical ties with India–and this, in turn, gives India a justification to be interested (and involved) in their well-being. The Sinhala majority, on the other hand, treat such ties suspect; the more so because of the fear that the huge population of neighbouring Tamil Nadu could any time cross the Palk Strait and reduce them into a minority in their own country. Hence every move for autonomy aiming at the ultimate creation of Tamil *Eelam* has to be crushed by the military–irrespective of the cost.

The same holds true about India's recently aroused interest in the well-being of the Tarai people–the Madhesias–in Nepal. Such interest, again, may have a justifiable basis, historical, cultural or otherwise; or democratic – such extra-territorial loyalties of the Madhesias could any time lead to secessionist pulls. A *Madhesi Eelam* in the Himalayas?

That because of its size and resources, India could exert influence on behalf of an ethnic minority having close ties with one or the other of its own linguistic and regional groups was made evident in the Indo-Sri Lanka Agreement signed by Rajiv Gandhi and J.R. Jayewardene in Colombo on July 29, 1987.[2] Defending the Agreement Rajiv Gandhi said in Parliament (July 31): "We have structured a framework for a durable solution to Sri Lanka's ethnic problem. The Agreement meets the basic aspirations which animated the Tamils struggle, namely, the desire to be recognized as a distinct ethnic entity, political autonomy for managing their political future, and appropriate devolution of governmental power to meet this objective", etc.[3]

Two Basic Assumptions Underlined

The above statement underlines two basic assumptions: First, India has a primary obligation to protect the rights of such minority communities in the neighbouring countries as have ties of kith and kinship with India, and second, majoritarian politics indeed have a baneful effect on the minorities in plural societies. The first assumption at once raises the issue whether India would be willing to allow its neighbours also to involve themselves in the affairs of communities (say Kashmir) whom they consider to be their own kith and kin? So far, India shows no inclination to accept such a thesis.

The second assumption stresses a general principle, viz., that *pluralistic societies minority groups must be allowed to develop their "distinct ethnic entity, political autonomy...* and devolution of governmental power". But this is a principle that the theme of "unity and integrity" of nation-state observes only by violation. A ruling establishment everywhere accumulates military, legal and other powers to simply crush demand for self-determination. The Centre wages war against the regions–Addis Ababa against Ogaden, Colombo against Jaffna, New Delhi against Punjab and Kashmir – to simply keep them under iron control. At the same time, since use of force itself generates uneasiness and fear among the neighbouring States, relations among nations deteriorate. The Tamil-Sinhala war led to heightening tensions, in fact great mutual acrimony, between India and Sri Lanka, India's use of force in Kashmir and Punjab brought about a near confrontation between New Delhi and Islamabad. And, the Ogaden war ignited an eight-year old armed conflict between Somalia and Ethiopia.

It is a pity that the ruling class in none of the post-colonial States has woken up to the danger of clinging wholly to the notion of nation-state – a notion which it imbibed from the West. Neither has anybody recognized the fact that no post-colonial State is homogeneous or unitary in the sense its ruling establishment would have us believe; but that it constitutes a plurality of different races, and communities with each having its identity rooted in separate custom, history, religion and language. This identity cannot be wished away whatever be the might of the State power or its insistence on building a strong, unified and secure nation. This is one simple lesson the African and Asian leaders have persistently refused to learn.

For a brief period, in the Marxist-run Nicaragua, the ruling circles applied their minds to analyse the roots of ethnic separatism, which they faced on the eastern coast. Their dialogue, Immanuel Ortega, raised the following points: (i) initially the Marxist Government refused oven to crush separatist demands by force; (ii) when this method failed, the Government provided schools, hospitals and other facilities to neutralize ethnic sentiments; even this failed; (iii) at the end, Ortega writes, the Marxists turned to the realization that ethnicity constitutes by itself a theoretical problem, which they need to study rather than simply ignore.[4]

It is unfortunate that Nicaraguan experiment was not allowed to develop into any kind of theoretical model. The 1989 elections intervened–and secured the defeat of Ortega's Marxist regime.

The ideology of nationalism and the Marxist construction of class conflict as the basis of social development have been extremely hostile to research into ethnic studies, which "is viewed with great suspicion as an attempt to promote disintegration and chaos in Third World societies".[5] Hence, notwithstanding the intensity of ethnic conflict in Africa or South Asia, the amount of research in this area remains very minimal. In recent years, the works of some Western Marxists such as Benedict Anderson and Ronaldo Munk have had limited impact on South Asian intellectuals. Their theories point to the fact that the resilience of nationalism and ethnicity in contemporary society reflects a failure of the left theory to use newer categories such as the nature of the state and the construction of political ideology.[6]

By this we do not mean the search for a symbiosis between nationalism and ethnicity, nor the populist glorification of marginalized communities with a dose of Gandhian morality. For neither approach admits of the larger role of ethnic identity at the national level. "There is a rejection of politicized ethnicity which would find expression in legal and administrative arrangements for the sharing of power at the national level. Therefore, the Sikh cause in India and the Tamil cause in the north and east of Sri Lanka are not accepted as valid. Pluralism, is not an end in itself".[7] Yet, if our research has to be meaningful, we must study ethnicity and ethnic identity as a category *per se*–and the one which *antecedates* the colonial category of nation-state. The later has led us nowhere except to greater political chaos, social disruption and violence. We must begin by rejecting this category before we make even the first move to understand historical and political patterns of identity formation in Third World societies.

NOTES

1. The title of a recent book published by Manchester University Press, 1991; edited by James Mayall and Anthony Payne, and in which the present author writes on "Paradise Lost: The Fall of Sri Lanka", pp.44-56.

2. For the text of the Agreement see Satish Kumar (ed.), Year book of India's Foreign Policy 1987-88, Sage, New Delhi, 1988, pp. 233-37.
3. *Ibid.*, pp. 238-39.
4. *Thatched Patio*, Colombo, 1988.
5. See Radhika Commaraswamy, "Race and Ethnic Studies: A South Asian Failure", *Thatched Patio*, August-September, 1987, p. 26.
6. *Ibid.*
7. *Ibid.*, p. 7.

3

ETHNICITY, NATION-STATE AND THIRD WORLD: A Critique of Critics

CHANDRAKALA PADIA

Ethnic conflicts today pose a growing threat to the unity of States. This is partly why some scholars have questioned the viability and legitimacy of nation-state as a representative of its people, and have recommended search for some other kind of political arrangement to accommodate the forces of ethnicity. The present paper aims at a critical examination of the validity of their objections to the very model of nation-state in the context of the Third World.

Before, however, I discuss these objections, it seems necessary to reflect on a commodity accepted definition of an ethnic group as "a collectivity within a larger society having real or putative common ancestry, memories of a shared historical past, and a cultural focus on one or more symbolic elements as the epitome of their nationhood".[1]

It is obvious that this definition aims at comprehensiveness. But I do not think it goes far enough. It only tells us what an ethnic group is, not how the group comes to be what it is. So I think it necessary to point out that the identity of an ethnic group becomes determinate, and comes to be acknowledged as such not only on the basis of what the members of the group in question share internally, but also as a result of conflict with other similar groups. Even generally, in real life, an individual or a nation is recognized as distinct partly on the basis of a comparative reference to other (different) individuals or nations. It is precisely because it does not provide for any such reference that the definition cited is to me incomplete. I believe that the concept of ethnicity is by no means wholly self-referrent.

In actual fact, however, ethnic groups are often labelled as anti-national; and so a question arises: Is this transition from the neutrality of ethnicity *as a concept* to its hostility *in practice* essential? Or does an ethnic group become anti-State because of some external reasons. I believe it is, by and large, some external factors which do the mischief. In itself ethnicity can be a quite legitimate expression of the democratic aspirations of a group without posing a threat to the unity of the State to which it belongs. It becomes a threat only when it is made to serve a narrow political end.

I may now turn to the critics of the very model of a nation-state. D.L. Sheth argues as follows:

> "The model of the nation-state is proving inappropriate for most Third World countries in solving their problems of ethnicity, as well as those of development ....dealing with a state-form which is primarily an out-growth of Western statecraft, and is based on a theory of state which invalidates their own experience of governance...(Earlier). The state was under the command of the society and not the other way round. Indeed, several political orders survived and competed with one another in these societies, in the past. But they were all subject to a larger civilizational order in which governance was not defined politically as a monopoly of the state. It was viewed as a primary structure of the social order, embedded in a civilizational society. The coming of the nation-states in these societies largely through forces exogenous to them turned their political and economic priorities upside-down. In the process of working with this new state-form, these societies lost their endogeneity."[2]

To facilitate understanding, the above quotation may be broken up into the following points:

1. Before the emergence of nation-states, the State was in a way controlled by society, and not *vice versa.*
2. The social order, then, was grounded in a common civilization and not determined by the State; and insofar as a civilization is a fabric of cultural forces, not an aggregate of political parties, it permitted pursuit of particular lifestyles in diverse ways, without any domination of one unit over another. To excel in one's own ways is not necessarily to dominate. To illustrate, in one and the same city, schools promoting different dance forms may well coexist without any conflict.
3. Since the structure of nation-states in the developing countries

automatically involved the concept of one political and cultural entity, and the participation of the whole nation in the matter of governance, the existing equations between different ethnic groups were disturbed. The various influential groups, on the basis of their intellectual or economic power, tried to monopolize State power, which led to politicization of ethnic groups of various kinds, each competing with the other.

Another unwholesome tendency in these nation-states which, according to Sheth, led to undesirable results was that the ruling elite became keener to join international organizations than to attend to more important internal matters. On becoming the official representatives of their respective nation-state at one or the other international forum, they started serving their own personal or group interests and remained concerned only about the juridical status of these new States, quite without caring whether they enjoyed legitimacy or not. Secondly, the elite agreed to participate in this international order on unequal terms, for they realized that their weak nation-states could not continue to exist without entering into agreements with, and subordinating their sovereignty, either politically or economically, to some developed nation. The result was that the old type of colonialism got replaced by a new one: externally by subordinating the interests of a country to those of the more developed ones; and internally by subjugating interests of ethnic minorities to those of ruling elite groups.[3]

Nation-State Model Not Invalidated

All these objections, however, though partially true, do not quite invalidate the "nation-state model" as a whole:

1. The fact that the State does not identify itself with society is not necessarily evil. For, it could be expected to work for a true and an objective assessment of the needs and problems of society and their proper redress. Historically, many a democratic nation-state has played a constructive role in the organization of society by liberating the individual from the petty tyrannies of local rulers, customs and religious authorities, restoring human liberty and dignity, fostering a sense of community among its diverse members, and ensuring equality and promoting a sense of mutual concern.

This is, however, not to deny that States, which were not conscious of their constructive role, bred narrow nationalism, limited citizens' sense of moral obligation to their own community, and fostered a statist manner of thinking. But this does not prove that a State is necessarily deficient in its institutional potential to act otherwise.

2. I submit that nation-states create problems only when they stay away from their ideal of ethnic neutrality and try to manipulate the aspirations of some select ethnic group to their own advantage. Many a State has recruited people for its law-enforcing machinery from one select group and has thus incited distrust in other groups. Let me illustrate. Countries like Thailand and Myanmar (Burma) which have adopted a mono-ethnic ideology by projecting only one group as their communal core have found it impossible to avoid organizing their entire political activity with an eye to showering benefits on the core community only. Contrarily, States like Singapore and quite a few in Black Africa with an ethnically *neutral* identity have developed national symbols utterly united to any particular cultural group, and have emphasized meritocratic ethnically neutral values. Here, what is more, the elites even try to *expose* the illegitimacy and subversive nature of merely ethnic affiliations.
3. Further, it may be a bit too sweeping and one-sided to blame the international order for ignoring the interests of ethnic groups. The truth rather is that now, due to an emerging international order, ethnic and other minorities can appeal beyond the jurisdiction of the State for the vindication of human rights and for other forms of protection. They may receive tacit or overt support from external forces identified as some of the superpowers. Indeed, it is becoming increasingly difficult for the nation-states to suppress the genuine demands of an ethnic minority by contending that such demands are matters of internal concern only.
4. I believe that the ethnic revival in the nation-state is in consonance with democratic values. Ethnic divisions have, in fact, existed since time immemorial; conflicts have been present (if only even implicitly), and grievances have been nursed for generations. It is only today that ethnic minorities can openly assert their claims with greater impunity just because they form a part of their nation-state; people can now openly claim their ethnic

> identities without any loss of self-esteem; they can even show they are proud of it and, in many cases, actively seek redress from perceived inequalities in terms of such identities, without being officially banned.

In fact, the very concept of nation-state provides legitimacy to ethnic groups, for it believes in the policy of self-determination. As Connor has forcefully argued, the trend has been forever smaller ethnically defined minorities to aspire to nationhood.[4] According to Smith, the spirit of nationalism is, in fact, what distinguishes the modern ethnic revival, pretty sharply from earlier ones; and on the other hand, the ideology of nationalism not only serves to legitimize truly national movements and aspirations, but also confers rationale and legitimacy on the typical recent claims for ethnic equality and pluralism within modern States.[5] Prof. Gore has also rightly argued: "Historically, the liberal nation-state has performed two important roles. It has facilitated the shift of political power closer to the citizen than ever before...(and) the organization of a polity with ethnic plurality; and (has) by so doing, enabled larger geographical units to be brought together in one State".[6]

Let me now turn to Ashis Nandy's basic objection to the concept of nation-state. "There is something in the nation-system that pushed it to split a culture into its high and its low components, to glorify the former and devalue the latter... High culture is...primarily the culture of the elites, with whom a functioning State has to establish at least a *quid pro quo*."[7]

Further, Nandy also tries to prove the validity of his argument in the context of India.

> "The nationalism that the Indian freedom movement left behind was a political as well as a powerful intellectual and cultural critique of the modern West. . . . All said, the nationalism India inherited was based on the idea of confederation. . . . That meaning of nationalism is now changing. There is now sizable number of Indians whom the new nationalists would love to call the true Indians. They are the modern Indians with a pan-Indian consciousness, fully committed to the culture of the nation-state, up-rooted from small local cultures, but having some access to the Indian high culture....The problems of national integration and ethnic violence in India have much to do with the distinction between the two forms of nationalism and the gradual loss of status of the in-

digenous form."[8]

Nandy's Contention Hardly Defensible

To my mind, Ashis Nandy's contention that contradictions are inherent in the very essence of a nation-state is hardly defensible. I believe that the nation-state is quite an accommodating model which can adjust itself to the individual character and major interests of different ethnic groups. And this is so because it has all the potential to work in consonance with democratic norms and values; to provide for the role of healthy traditional forces; and yet to accommodate modernity. Nandy has, however, overlooked the possibility that the enlightened individuals of all ethnic groups can be expected to contain the anti-democratic forces of ethnicity.

In fact, instead of finding fault with the model of nation-state, the right course would be to emphasize the creation of conditions for the development of the human aspect of individual personality, so as to provide a check against the tendency towards ethnocentrism. We should also remember that no model, howsoever democratic it may sound, can work in a kind of vacuum, and without the help of right-minded endeavour. For "no provision is by itself an active force. It is merely the offer of a facility."[9]

Moreover, whatever be the political model that we ultimately decide to choose, whether it be that of the nation-state as at present understood, or that of a loose federation of ethnic groups each enjoying freedom in the preservation of its cultural mores and coming together only when the need arises to face some external aggression, our basic, if implicit, concern cannot but be the happiness of the human individual. This is the basic fact from which all political thinking has to begin and which has ever to be borne in mind; but it is precisely this which is generally ignored in our abstract discussions about the nature of an ideal political model. And if, we start from a clear recognition of the supreme importance of human happiness, the natural development of thought would, in my view, take the following course:

The happiness of an individual depends, significantly even if in part, upon the harmony of his relations with his environment, both human and natural. No person can be happy in a kind of isolation or vacuum. Everyone has to get along with others, and so may have to curtail one's own individual freedom for the welfare of people around one. What is more, if one is to enjoy the facilities of fresh air and clean drinking water, one must also do one's duty by way of abstaining from polluting physical environment. And a little education is enough to make one see the truth of all this. But if an individual can be so made to put a little check on his individual living, why cannot a whole ethnic group be expected to respond similarly to the influence of education. So, I would suggest that instead of accepting the model of a loose federation of ethnic groups as suggested by Prof. Nandy, a suggestion which seems to ignore the very possibility of self-discipline through education, the better way would be to work for the idea of a more cohesive nation-state by educating the various ethnic groups with a view to making them see that some curtailment of individual ethnic liberty in almost every direction may be demanded by the overall interests of the nation by which I understand the maximum possible happiness of every individual member of the nation.

NOTES

1. R.A. Schermerhorn, *Comparative Ethnic Relations*, New York, Random House, 1970, p. 12. Also see: Nathan Glazer and Daniel P. Moynihan (ed.), *Ethnicity: Theory and Experience*, Cambridge, Harvard University Press, 1975; Joseph Rothschild, *Ethnopolitics: A Conceptual Frame-work*, New York, Columbia University Press, 1981; Donald L. Horwitz, *Ethnic Groups in Conflict*, Berkeley, University of California Press, 1985.
2. D.L. Sheth, "State, Nation and Ethnicity: Experience of Third World Countries", *Economic and Political Weekly*, March 25, 1989, p. 625. Also see a revised version of this article entitled "Nation-Building in Multi-Ethnic Societies: The Experience of South Asia", *Alternatives*, Vol. XIV, 1989, pp. 379-388.
3. D.L. Sheth, "State, Nation and Ethnicity", p. 620.
4. See, W. Connor, "Ethnonationalism in the First World: the present in historical perspective" in M. Esmar (ed.) *Ethnic Conflict in the Western World*, Ithaca and London, Cornell University Press, 1977.
5. See, A.D. Smith, *The Ethnic Revival in the Modern World*, Cambridge, Cambridge University Press, 1981.
6. M.S. Gore, "India and the Concept of the Nation-State", Sri Purushottamdas Thakurdas Memorial Lecture on Monday December 11, 1989, p. 2 (a leaflet).
7. Ashis Nandy, "The Political Culture of the Indian State", *Daedalus*, Journal of the American Academy of Arts and Science, Fall, 1989.
8. Ibid., p. 12, 13, 14.
9. See, Iqbal Narain and Chandrakala Padia, "Commentary on Fred. W. Riggs' A Neoinstitutional Typology of Third World Politics" in Anton Bebler and Jim Seroka, *Contemporary Political Systems*, Boulder and London, Lynne Rienner Publishers, 1990, p.241.

4

CHALLENGE OF ETHNICITY AND NATION-BUILDING

SACHCHIDANANDA

Ethnicity is a ubiquitous phenomenon in both developing and developed countries, past and present. In the Third World, tribes and communities are becoming integral parts of new State structures and are thus being transformed into ethnic groups with varying degrees of cultural distinctiveness. Social scientists have been forced into dealing with socio-cultural and political problems raised by the developing interdependence or the rising tension between these parts and by the processes of socio-cultural change involved in this development. Because of its ubiquity, variety of form, scope and intensity and of its involvement in psychic, social and historical variables, ethnicity has been defined in a variety of ways.

An ethnic group can be operationally defined as a collectivity of people who share same patterns of normative behaviour and form a part of larger populations interacting with people from other collectivities within the framework of a social system. The term ethnicity refers to the degree of conformity by members of the collectivity to these shared norms in the course of social interactions.

Ethnicity is thus essentially a form of interaction between cultural groups operating in a social context. It is a complex problem as it involves a number of sociological, historical, economical and political factors. Some authorities explain ethnicity in terms of motivation, primordial idea or the psychology of identity. Ethnicity is ultimately connected with economic and political relationships. Political relations are construed not in the narrow sense in which the political scientists use it, but in the social sense in which politics becomes the manipulation of power at any level. Sometimes ethnicity is expressed through cultural mechanisms to articulate the feelings and aspirations of distinctive groups. It is in such situations that political ethnicity surfaces. Many deprived groups–racial, religious, linguistic and regional – begin to opt for a solution which the democratic polity leaves open to them. In many areas there have been minority agitations directed towards a solution of its power deprivation through direct or indirect methods and through violent or constitutional means. Agitations have been organized around various kinds of pursuits and demands such as complete separation from the existing State, regional autonomy, equality of representation at the centres of power, equality of economic opportunities and special guarantees and safeguards for religion, language and culture.

Ethnicity is a highly charged and emotive issue and easily lends itself to mobilization by interested parties. Those who stand to gain through this revive discarded primordialities and resurrect beyond symbols. Earlier the concept of homogenization in which the world has been conceived as a global village was gaining momentum. The message was for one humanity and one planet. However, the sudden outburst of the ethnic phenomenon was a disturbing experience and reversed the move towards homogenization. Since the eighties ethnic assertion has been growing. Ethnicity is no longer confined to its estymological meaning. Ethnic identity subsumes much more. Its main ingredients are (a) common descent, (b) socially relevant cultural or physical characteristics, (c) set attitudes and behavioural patterns, (d) religion and (e) language. The ethnic group is also characterized by "We" and "They" feeling. These are also efficient mechanisms for boundary maintenance. There are two approaches to the issue, one based on common descent and the other is situational or subjectivist/instrumental. It is based on the members' perception of being different from others. Ethnicity involves consolidation, mobilization, goal-setting and goal attainment. It eludes a standard definition. It is part sentiment, part ideology and part agenda.[2]

Worldwide Resurgence of Ethnicity

The resurgence of ethnicity is a worldwide. It is seen in the growing demands of the American Indians and their continuing pressure on the U.S. administration for conceding their superseded rights, their pride in their own culture and their attempts to arrest assimilationist tendencies. The demand of the Scottish people for a separate legislature for Scotland is another example. The movement of the Basque on the Franco-

Spanish border for a homeland of their own and the dismemberment of Yugoslavia are other examples of the same phenomenon. Ethnic issues were also extremely important in the breaking up of the erstwhile USSR. Earlier we had thought that ethnic issues had been satisfactorily solved by an efficient management in the Soviet system. In India itself the ethnic upsurge has long plagued the North-East. By slow degrees, in the course of two decades, many States were formed out of Assam. Even now there are demands for the creation of Udayachal and Bodoland. Karbi Anglong and Silcher people are also agitating for separate statehood. In West Bengal the Gorkhaland agitation led to the grant of a new constitutional status for Darjeeling. In Bihar the Jharkhand movement is moving towards a showdown and some solution has to be found for satisfying its demands. In Uttar Pradesh there is agitation for the setting up of a new State of Uttarakhand. Similarly Vidarbha is wanting a separate identity for itself. In many ways the Punjab problem may also be reckoned as an ethnic issue.

It will be useful at this stage to review the socio-economic and political developments in the Third World countries in the second half of the present century. In the beginning all efforts were geared to win political freedom and throw off the colonial rule. Once freedom was attained the leadership went all out for economic development so as to catch up with the developed countries. Thus involved modernization not only of technology but also a social and cultural life. It was felt that the pattern of development adopted accentuated socio-economic inequalities. Thus efforts were made to usher in social equality and to emphasize social and distributive justice. When this could not be achieved in full measure for the different communities in the nation-state, demands emerged for cultural self-determination. This further led to assertion of ethnic identities.

Besides this, there are several contributing factors to the growth of ethnicity. The more important of these are discussed below. The cultural arrogance of the dominant population over tribal communities is deeply resented by them. The cultural assault is manifested through division of their way of life on the ground that it was primitive, callous neglect of their language and traditions, domination over the religious and social mores, etc. Domination, subordination and exploitation of specific communities led to a feeling of alienation among them. In their own homeland the tribals were reduced to a subordinate status whereas outsiders continue to occupy position of power, influence and wealth. They are also the instruments of economic exploitation. They not only monopolize employment but also trade and commerce in the region.[3]

The ethnic communities are highly apprehensive of the erosion of their culture and identity. They fear that in course of time they will be crushed under the roller of the culture of the dominant community and would lose their identity. This sometimes makes them highly ethnocentric and they make it a point to cling to some distinctive features in their life and culture. Besides this some communities feel that they are denied social and distributive justice by the dominant community and they have to fight for equity and for their entry into the portals of power. They want a share in decision-making. They want to be masters of their own destiny. In recent times, foreign powers inimical to the States stroke the fires of ethnicity. Bangladesh and Pakistan have been doing this in Assam, Tripura and Kashmir and Punjab respectively. They provide funds, arms and training to the insurgent groups. Sometimes the ethnic card is used to maintain political leadership of regional parties or individuals. The ethnic group is a volatile constituency for their political support.

Ethnicity is a challenge to major paradigms of development. It has defied both Communist and non-Communist manifestoes. Efforts made by them could not contain the assertion of ethnic identities. It has been realized that participative development is possible only in smaller units.

Ethnicity works as a factor for fusion within the context of the group and also as measure for distinction and differentiation between groups. Peterson[4] observes that the worldwide rise of ethnicity is based on the quest for community and more importantly for the wider functions of the State. It generated greater impetus to organize in order to get what the State is now distributing and to prevent others from getting it. Some aspects of ethnicity appear to be disruptive and opposed to national integration. This may not be necessarily so if the potential of ethnic identities is mobilized in a thoughtful and constructive way. This may be done by according a measure of recognition and autonomy for all the nationalities and ethnic groups. The State should try to curb the cultural arrogance of the dominant community. It should be responsive to cultural differences existing between different communities. It is also necessary to promote the participation of all the ethnic communities in the working of all national institutions. There should be no evidence of prejudice and discrimination, direct or indirect, in any State action. It is good that in India reverse discrimination has been adopted as State policy to better the lot of the poor and hitherto deprived and neglected communities. Although the policy has not affected all sections of the Scheduled Castes, Scheduled Tribes and other backward communities to an equal extent, its fruits are slowly spreading out.

No Integration without Participation

It is evident that we cannot have perfect social and emotional integration of different communities in India without giving them an effective participation in the national polity. Through the Constitution we have given to all communities equal rights but, in fact, the equality of opportunities does not obtain for all communities or for different sections of the same community. Thus there can be no integration without participation. Efforts should be made to see that this participation is effective at different levels for most of the people.

In India we have a multi-layered society. In this we must provide for appropriate degrees of autonomy, to meet the socio-political aspirations of different communities. An interdependent societal pattern may satisfy the demands of the Indian situation rather than a uniform pattern for all areas and people. Thus through better understanding, acceptance and appreciation of ethnic distinctiveness, its disruptive potential can be curbed and turned into an instrument of creative action.

NOTES

1. Cohen, Abner, "The Lesson of Ethnicity" in Abner Cohen (ed.), *Urban Ethnicity*, Tavistock Publications, London, 1974.
2. Dube, S.C., Inaugural address to IPRA Seminar on Ethnic Identities and Social Transformation, Chandigarh, 1990.
3. Sachchidananda, Ethnicity as a Political Force in Chota Nagpur, presented at the Seminar on Ethnic Identities and Social Transformation, Chandigarh, 1990.
4. Peterson, "Ethnicity in the World Today" in *International Journal of Comparative Sociology*, Vol. XX (1 and 2), 1979.

5

ETHNIC IDENTITY AND NATIONAL INTEGRATION IN INDIA

L.N. SHARMA

It is much too apparent for anybody to see that vast populations not only in Asia, Africa and Latin America but even in the erstwhile USSR are steeped in tradition and owe allegiance to traditional bonds based, among others, on "parochial" ethnic identities. It is also true that in many of them, State power in a bid to modernize the system tried to break the hold of traditional pluralities and advanced the argument that it was necessary to do so in order to ensure a modern, united, prosperous and powerful polity. Not all political engineers of analysts are agreed, however, in thinking that persistence of ethnic identities is antithetical to the nation-state. Rajni Kothari, among others, argues that tradition and culture contribute to the acquisition of depth and resilience to a democratic polity.[1]

The issue, however, is not that ethnic identities exist and may be allowed to exist but that acute political mobilization on the basis of ethnic separateness or exclusiveness assumes dimensions of serious conflict, leading to arson, violence and terrorism undermining the integrative capabilities of the system. In this paper, we examine the issue of ethnic identities and national integration in the context of India in three broad historical phases and try to draw lessons from them for modern times.

The Ancient (Aryan) Period

Diverse ethnic and religious groups came in succession and settled down in India since the most ancient times. India's style of integrating them was, however, eclectic rather than proselytizing. This made coexistence of diverse system and lifestyles possible. At the same time, it led to persistence of local subcultures and primary loyalties particularly because the governmental centre was intermittent, unstable and discontinuous. In contrast to the historical empires of the West, the unity of India owed itself not to other authority of a given political system but to the wide diffusion of the cultural symbols, the spiritual values and the structure of roles and functions characteristic of a continuous civilization. India was known more for her cultural than for her political identity.

Kautilya's *Arthashastra* brilliantly brings forth the point that India's culture had a secular component. *Manusmriti*, on the other hand, symbolizes the spiritual component. But an important point to note is that through a constant interplay between the secular and the spiritual components, the system adapted itself to changing situations. There has been cross-cutting between the secular and the spiritual components of civilization but no ecclesiastical-temporal battles characteristic of the West.

For a large part, alliances between the political and priestly figures provided the mechanism of Indian society's absorptive capacity. But within the parameters of this alliance, segmented change was possible. While too much aggregation was avoided, ethnic identities were freely retained. The whole picture adds up to the tolerance of various cultural and religious diversities. Through an all-pervasive caste system, various tribal and semi-tribal people, different religious sects, and invading and immigrant groups were integrated into a common cultural and secular framework. There were movements like the *Bhakti* movement which brought Sikhs into being and in the context of the times in which that movement arose, it provided further unity and not division. Thus the Buddhists, Jains, Sikhs and Hindus lived together as if they were part of one nation.

The Muslim Period

The Muslims confronted the Hindus with a different religion and social system. The Arabs, Afghans and Mongols came as raiders and conquerors. Although as rulers, many of them wanted the Hindus and the Muslims to live together in amity, religious conversions became attractive, especially in the north. Oftentimes this led to repression, religious bigotry and hatred on both sides. Social assimilation of the earlier period received a serious jerk. There are instances of adjustments and mutual influences between the two communities but the two religious and social systems remained separate and mutually exclusive. Hindu suffered from a sense of defeat and humiliation.

The Hindu-Muslim relationship, however, has passed through several stages. During the period of Muslim ascendancy, a feeling of estrangement and hostility prevailed between leaders of the two communities, in spite of a general mutual acceptance of each other at the level of ordinary people. During the period following, under early British rule, Hindus and Muslims learnt to live side by side, grew tolerant of each other, carved out distinctive spheres of influence and occupation, and participated in many common activities. There came about a worsening of the situation, however, during the latter period of the British rule, through a cumulation of cleavages at the national level. Hindu revivalism, and Westernization went side by side.

The British Impact

The 1857 revolt was joined by many Muslim princely and landed families that had been shorn of their power by the all-encroaching British, though a large number of Hindu rulers also joined in. The Britishers adopted an anti-Muslim posture in the period just following the revolt but, by the last decades of the nineteenth century, started playing one against the other. During the same period Hindu revivalism also made a dent. Even during the twentieth century, Tilak and Gandhi did not reject the religious basis of nationalism and drew inspiration from tradition for political action. Gandhi's fast against "Communal Award" and his efforts to avoid partition showed the value that he attached to unity. However, the British Government, the Congress and the political leadership of the Muslims contributed in their own way to the growing alienation and hostility among the Hindus and Muslims. The British rule had also contributed to the unequal development of Muslims and in a way to Hindu revivalism and Muslim adverse reaction against it.

Numerical strength and organized political action got a premium due to elections. Politicians mobilized ethnic groups and identities. In place of the old nationalist ideology in which the expression of the caste communal identity in politics was frowned upon and a separate political organization for minorities was counteracted, the new strategy was to rely on minority vote banks. Movement has not been towards the growth of a political national secular community but towards the maintenance of ethnic identities for parochial and sectarian purpose.

What is needed is to accelerate eco-development of various regions and sections of the population to tone down ethnic conflicts while social movements are required to see that ethnic identities are not encouraged to aggregate unnecessarily.

NOTE

1. Rajni Kothari, *State Against Democracy: In Search of Humane Governance*, Delhi: Ajanta, 1988, p. 156.

6

IDENTITY OF INDIAN MUSLIMS AND PROBLEMS OF NATIONAL INTEGRATION

MOHD. SHOWEB

India is a multi-ethnic society and it comprises different religious groups and sub-cultures. This diversity is an asset and creates a beautiful mosaic of culture, yet, it has created a complex problem for nation-building. The Constitution has visualized the creation of secular society, yet, the experiences of the past four decades show that there are serious problems of conflict in the country. Each ethnic group though participating in the nation-building process wants to preserve its own socio-cultural identity. Moreover, there are attempts to extend the socio-cultural hegemony of the dominant ethnic groups over others. Now here, the conflict and dissension can be found more rampant than in the case of Muslims who constitute the dominant minority of Indian society.

The problem of integration of Muslims in Indian society can be analysed from different perspectives. It can be analysed from the angle of Muslim identity. Much has been said about the historical and political aspect of the problem but here I would like to confine myself to the socio-cultural dimension of the problem.

The assertion of Muslim identity has deep socio-cultural anchors. Islam is the pervasive element in the social organization of Muslim community. The community identifies itself very closely with the precepts and practices of Islam. But the religiosity of the Muslim has created many problems. On the one hand Muslims are divided into different sects, apart form the dominant *Shia-Sunni* sect; the majority *Sunni* is further subdivided into *Barelvis, Deobandis* and *Ahle-Hadith.* Each sect interprets Islam in its own way. This has created a conflict within the Muslim community. The reaction of each sect towards every basic national issue is different depending upon the political patronage and benefits. The Muslim community which is theoretically called a monolithic one has in fact wide pluralistic tendencies. Thus, when the question of integration of Muslims in the national mainstream is analysed, the pluralistic characteristics should also be taken into consideration.

The identification of the Muslim community has created another problem in terms of identity formation. Generally it is believed that Islam is one and same everywhere. The global and universal characteristics of Islam are very much emphasized. But a deep probe into the social structure of Islam in any country would reveal its regional characteristics. These are a reflection of the process of indigenous religious traditions. Islam as practised in different parts of the globe reflects wide variation. Even in India the religious beliefs and customs of Muslims belonging to different regions is different. This has created many problems of adjustment within the Muslim society. Those who adhere to the basic fundamentals of Islam would treat the indigenous traits of Islam as un-Islamic and, therefore, they advocate their withdrawal. On the other hand the Muslim masses treat them as age-old customs and would cling to it. This can be seen in the form of conflicts in *Barelvi, Deobandi* and *Ahle-Hadith* sects especially in North India. The Muslims find themselves in a dilemma. Identification with local tradition contributes to integration of Muslim community with Indian soil but it is considered un-Islamic by the "Ulemas". Thus it is clear that Islam which gives a special cultural identity to Muslims is itself passing through a crisis and, therefore, the problem of Muslim identity is confused.

Apart from the religious dimensions of the identity formation we can now look towards the linguistic aspect of the problem. Urdu has come to be identified as the language of Muslims. The North Indian Muslims speak Urdu and would like to have their children learn it so that the cultural continuity of the community may remain intact. However, the all-India perspective of the problem indicates that in each region of the country Muslims speak different languages. For example, Malayali Muslims in Kerala share many more things with Malayali Hindus than those who share with a Muslim from Assam or Bihar. This adoption of regional language by Muslims has created significant consequences. Regional language and dialects have contributed to a closer interaction between Muslims and non-Muslims in a particular region. Thus the linguistic identity of the Muslim community should not be equated with the all-India status of Urdu only. In fact the

Muslim community in India is multi-lingual and identifies closely with regional languages.

Muslim Community Not Monolithic

Any study of Indian Muslims can very well reveal that the community is not a monolithic one as it is perceived by the outsiders. In fact, the Muslim community is multi-ethnic, multi-lingual, multi-sectoral and comprises different sub-cultures. Therefore, to define the identity of the Muslim community in terms of socio-cultural processes is a difficult task. At the level of socio-cultural dynamics several identities exist which are sometime mutually congruent while at others they create dissonance and dissensions in the system.

A few words about the class structure of the Muslim community in India can also be added to understand the process of identity formation. Islam, though preaches egalitarianism and is against all distinction based on birth, ancestry, etc., yet, the socio-structural Islam in India is quite repugnant to this principle. Caste-like groupings and invisible hierarchy are found among them. "Ashraf" and "Ajlaf" are the two broad categories where the distinctions have been made between the higher and the lower caste. Middle and lower-rank castes are very much strict about endogamous marriages. Thus, within the Muslim community rigid stratification based on ascriptive criteria of birth is becoming strong. On the other hand the community is divided into different economic strata-landed aristocracy, businessmen, shopkeepers, artisans and manual labourers are the major divisions. Educated middle class with salaried employment is a very small group. Thus, the economic interest of each occupational group is different. It inhibits the ability of the community to form a homogeneous economic group. Thus, the Muslim community in India presents a scenario which gives the community many sub-identities. The federal characteristic of the community should be, therefore, properly understood while exploring the process of identity formation of the Muslim community in India.

The fact of internal pluralism among the Muslims is important not only in understanding the nature of the community, but also its integration with the nation and the State. Muslims are primarily concerned with their constitutional rights of security of life and property, equality of opportunity in education and services, and freedom of trade and enterprise. They accept the demand for integration and participate in all walks of life as equal citizens. They, however, reject the demand for uniformity of laws and institutions in socio-cultural spheres as necessary condition for national unity. They accept India as their homeland but resent political invasion of their religious and cultural rights to meet the unnecessary and unreasonable demands of parochial nationalism.

7

ETHNICITY, INDIAN NATIONAL IDENTITY AND NATIONAL INTEGRATION

M.G. HUSAIN and SUSHMA SURI

From time immemorial Indian civilization remained important which attracted global attention. The warriors, the adventurists, the religious preachers, etc., came to this land and stayed and also accepted it as their homeland. Irrespective of their origins they contributed to progress and development of this country. The heterogeneity of their heritage did not prevent them from unifying the socio-cultural roots and assimilating with local customs and civilization. This might be the reason why the rulers in the past did not have people from any single religious sect in their governments or armies. Akbar the great had a Rajput general, Shivaji had a Muslim one and Maharaja Ranjeet Singh too had Muslim lieutenants.

In spite of the fact that India is a plural society it produced a unique integrated culture based on different religions like Hinduism, Buddhism, Islam, Christianity, Sikhism, etc. Although different people embraced different religions their language, style of living, values, etc., were not divided on these grounds. In India ethnic groups are formed through various criteria such as religion, caste, region, language, socio-economic status, etc. Thus ethnicity denotes those characteristics of a society which is bound together by the concept of race or community or groups with an identity of its own. Primarily, it is social product-based on cultural and social content or patterns. Now-a-days it is used for a feeling given by a racial, social, cultural and psychological consciousness. Thus, the members of each ethnic group have certain opinions, ideas and attitudes of their own as well as about the members of other groups and the feeling of "we group" and "they group" becomes imminent.

Ethnic groups are inherently ethnocentric regarding their own cultural trait as natural, correct and superior to those of other ethnic groups who are perceived as odd, amusing, inferior or immoral. Nationality, language, religion and tribal identity are all ethnic categories that have been employed to distinguish between conflicting groups. The duration as well as the origin and span of ethnic stratification is commonly influenced by adaptive capacity. Once people have become a minority, flexibility on their part is essential for the sake of equality. Inequality of power is defining the characteristics of dominant and minority groups. Majority-minority relations do not appear strained until one group successfully impose its will upon others. Once ethnic differences have been perceived the ethnic groups begin to compete against each other. Hence the most important variable is the differential power of one group in relation to another. These basic differences appear in terms of perception of people belonging to different religions, regions, castes and linguistic groups. This denotes how they use themselves, people of other groups, their practices, languages, social behaviour and roles in the nation.

Ignorance Cause of Mutual Prejudices

The reorganization of States, lack of acceptance of one national language, regional disparities, vote catching strategies by manipulating majority vs minority feelings and above all failure to develop a national identity, strong social identity could be believed as some of the fact leading to the heightening tension, communalism, segregation, etc., instead of unification. In India and elsewhere in the world the ethnic identities begin to emerge very early in childhood and crystallize during early adolescence. Several Indian studies on the development of religion and caste identities have confirmed this (Jabbi, 1981; Khan 1979; Prasad, 1973; Sharma, 1986; Husain and Suri, 1989). On the basis of their study Suri and Husain found very high religious identity among Muslim and Sikh children than among their Hindu counterparts. The results of a series of studies carried out by the authors have depicted that both Muslim and Sikh minorities were having a very strong cultural, religious and linguistic identity and a relatively weaker national identity as compared to their majority counterparts. The Scheduled Caste subjects showed equally stronger trend of national and religious identity as caste Hindus. However, their linguistic and cultural identity were the weakest. It was also observed that the level of prejudice in Muslim and Sikh children was relatively higher than in Hindus (Singh, 1980). Many other studies have also indicated that other majority of Muslims in India are economically and educationally backward. There are various reasons of their backwardness. As a matter of fact Muslim community experiences economic hardship due to the rigid adherence to their family trades and business. This cannot be accepted fully as they fail to get equal opportunities in different walks of life. The socio-cultural constraint are also responsible for their economic backwardness. But Muslims commonly believe that their economic and educational backwardness is due to discrimination practised against them. However, it is believed that our mutual prejudices are the result of our lack of information about each other. Lack of authentic information even among the educated sections of society, misinformations, deliberate or otherwise, result in strengthening prejudices against the others.

Religion does influence cultural processes too. Culture is a very complex entity and cannot be reduced to one single factor like religion. Some religion produces a variety of cultures if other elements vary. Such as Kashmiri Muslim culture, North Indian Muslim culture, Punjabi Muslim culture, Bengali Muslim culture etc. Similarly, Hindu culture is also being used as a monolithic concept which is problematic too. There is no such thing as monolithic all-India Hindu culture one can identify with. There are Bengali, Kashmiri, North Indian, Tamil, Assamese and Punjabi cultures. There is one more problem with Hindu culture. It is caste-ridden, what passes off as "Hindu Culture" is in fact upper-caste Brahamanical culture. The "Shudras" or "Dalits" can hardly take pride in this upper-caste culture. Thus cultural identity does not embody any unique properties, rather it is a set of processes which can totally account for the differences we observe.

It is observed that religious or cultural identity acquires an added significance when threat to identify is universally manifested. The Indian Hindus and Muslims or Pakistani Hindus or Pakistani Muslims are more Westernized in their attitude and behaviours than the Hindu and Muslims of the U.K. or the USA. Today in India Hindu identity is being aggressively asserted on others to assimilate themselves with this "Hindu identity". As a result this creates a situation wherein the minorities too tend to assert their identity equally aggressively and thus the confrontation acquires its own momentum. Political confrontation encourages religio-culture confrontation and that in turn strengthens political confrontation. The "Babri Masjid-Ramjanambhumi," issue is a symbol of this which is becoming more and mor: deep-rooted.

Almost all ethnic groups are interlocked in bitter and violent conflicts. The rich and the poor in all parts of the country, the Hindus and the Muslims in several parts, the Hindus and the Sikhs in Punjab, the tribals and the non-tribals in Bihar and the Christians and non-Christians in Kerala. Formation of minority group identifies their group images, their attitudes toward other social groups and their socio-political behaviour too is very much responsible for ethnic stratification (Singh, 1986). Relative deprivation has been suggested as a factor conducive to inter-group tension (Naqvi, 1982; Tripathi and Srivastava, 1980). The rise in aspiration as well as political consciousness in the socially disadvantaged groups are likely to intensify the feeling of relative deprivation.

A.K. Singh's review of literature on "Inter-group relations and social tension in India" revealed that inter-group tension in India is being increasingly explained more by socio-economic factors and less by religious factors. The importance of economic equality, demand for social justice, an assumption for political rights and so on have been considered by many authors. The increasing trend of such diversities is really a curse for the development of the nation. Thus in this conflicting situation national integration is the basic need to reconcile these conflicts. Emotional integration involves the acceptance of a common and consistent set of values, norms and attitudes by all sections of the people. In India, although political integration has largely been achieved, emotional integration is still a distant dream. The reasons are not only the size, economy or diversity of this country. There are certain socio-psychological constraints as mentioned above. In order to reconcile these concepts based on religious, caste, cultural, regional, economical and political interests we have to tackle the problem of national integration in terms of a genuine secular approach which keeps various diversified groups in the fabric of single nation. Indian culture is not unitary culture rather it is composite culture. The only thread that binds the people of varying castes, creeds and languages in the fabric of one nation is the feeling of belongingness.

National Integration a Two-fold Process

National integration is a social, psychological and educational process through which a feeling of unity, solidarity and cohesion develops in the heart of the people and a sense of common citizenship and a feeling of loyalty to the nation is among them. It is a process of creation of a common bond together with a strong feeling of brotherhood. In other words, national integration may be conceived as a two-fold process with administrative and political integration on the one hand and emotional integration on the other. The latter is relatively more permanent.

National integration has been defined differently by different theorists in many ways. Weiner (1965) distinguished between five uses of the term integration:

(1) 1. the integration of diverse and discrete cultural loyalties,
(2) 2. territorial integration,
3. value integration,
4. elite-mass integration,
5. the integration of individuals in the organization for purposive activity. Political integration is said to be complete when the majority of the people of a country accept its administrative network and abide by its law and emotional integration involving the acceptance of a common and consistent set of values, norms and attitudes by all sections of the people.

As described earlier the majority, the ruling groups, rich, dominant sections always try to impose their will upon the minority, the poor and so on. This conscious or unconscious effort to suppress the weaker groups provokes them to resent, and the eruption is in many forms such as political changes, caste and communal tensions, revolt against the Government and police, demand for regional autonomy/separate homeland, etc. Minor types of suppression lead to many reactions and finally result in the form of larger conflicts. Instead of reconciliation these prolong indefinitely. Such types of conflicts sometimes become causes of terrorist activities. The unlawful elements rise against the Government and other ethnic groups. State uses force to suppress the anti-social elements with equal terrorist tactics. There are reports which reveal that these forces' (Police-PAC) action and attitude are highly partisan towards the minorities and weaker sections.

Similarly, organized political groups in power always attempt to eliminate or render their rival political organizations ineffective. In this process they forget everything and use all moral-immoral, legal-illegal, proper-improper means to achieve their goals. This type of "terrorism" further alienates the ethnic groups which assert for their rights. The so-called terrorism is not practised by anti-social elements alone against the society and Government. The Government's dealing with the minority group is, as a matter of fact, a kind of terrorism in practice. Likewise there is another sign of a worse attitude of political terrorism when any Government of regional party which comes in power is dismissed only because it does not toe the line of the major political party which holds the balance of power. This act is certainly a sort of political terrorism against our own people. This may not allow them to be loyal to the nation, and their frustration and anger may corrode their love for their fellow countrymen. The Indian national identity–loyalty of Indians towards their nation–does not clash with ethnic identity. One should accept national identity above any sub-national identity or social identity and its components.

The Indian national identity has to be built on the commonness of all Indians. Different sub-identities based on religion, caste, ethnicity etc. do not provide any basis for any commonness. Ethnicity and ethnocentrism simply create feelings of in-group and out-group affiliations. These categorizations have to be ignored for making a larger platform for building a stronger Indian national identity.

Sociologists and psychologists tend to stress the fact that a sense of identity is formed from the dialectics between the individual and society: identity are formed, maintained and modified by social processes (Berger and Luckmann, 1966). According to Gergen the social and personal identity are hypothetical cognitive structure. For him social identity components are nationality, religion, political application and so on whereas personal identity is solely concerned with one's self. For Tajfel social identity is individual's knowledge that he belongs to certain groups together with some emotional and value significance to him of that group membership. Knowledge of group membership is achieved through the process and divides his social world into categories and classes. The categorization helps the individuals to strive to develop and maintain a positive sense of social identity. This further helps/forces him to make comparison with other groups.

Individuals who are members of groups that suffer inferior social status cannot avail themselves of the above options. Most minority groups are a case in point, racial and ethnic minorities more particularly so. Membership of a minority group entails the social consequences of being unlike the majority. The majority comprises any group that in a salient situation holds the balance of power and resources.

1. Minorities are subordinate segments of complex State societies.
2. Minorities have special physical or cultural traits which are held in low esteem by the dominant segments of society.
3. Minorities are self-conscious units bound together by special traits which their members share and by special disabilities that these traits bring.
4. Membership in a minority is transmitted by rule of descent which is capable of affiliating succeeding generations even in the absence of readily apparent special culture or physical traits.
5. Minority people by choice or necessity tend to marry within the group.

The ethnic identities of minority groups are questioned quite often. Members of minority groups feel alienated and threatened when they come closer to an alien group. This is because the majority fails to accept him as a separate group and wants them to assimilate into their folds. The minority, on the other hand, does not accept this and face a situation of mutual suspicion.

As regards the political status of minorities they hardly feel themselves very comfortable. The presumption is that they hail from a low social strata. This class difference and other facts put them on war path or confrontation with others on the basis of class and ethnicity. Besides, they become subject to discrimination – real or perceived. Discrimination can be perceived according to the universal norms like equality, freedom, justice and the like. A discriminating society forces minorities into segregation by having parallel institutions like schools and other organizations. Their political assimilation is made in the name of political ideology which in fact is directed at destroying minority groups as a collective force or entity (UNESCO Joint Study, 1977). This has also been strengthened by the observations of Mascovici and Paicheler (1978) that a minority is denied social equality due to repressive segregation. This political segregation has a two-fold aim of providing social equality and social recognition. The conditions of discrimination and political assimilation, i.e. denial of equal opportunity, leads to an over-identification with a minority ethnic group and under-identification with a majority group which are as a matter of fact a defensive process expressing psychological uncertainty and feelings of threat (Mascovici and Paicheler). According to Lauren (1973) and Reinans (1973) disproportionate representation of minority youths becomes the cause of identity disturbance.

A minority group, especially ethnic minority, has over-estimation of its size (perceived size), equality, culture, value, etc. This is more pertinent when it is categorized (social categorization) in terms of race, religion, language and sex, Tajfel conceptualized this categorization as a function of stereotype and prejudice.

National Identity is Crumbling

In spite of negligence and discrimination the ethnic minorities have contributed to nation-building in many ways. Thus the problem of national integration is not of the minorities alone, it rather concerns all. In the present Indian context it is strongly felt that larger sections of our countrymen do not bother to bring minorities into the mainstream by developing an Indian national identity. In the recent years the social situations witnessed indicate that instead of being strengthened the national identity is crumbling due to social injustice, discrimination, politicization of minor social issues, imposition of majority will upon others and so on. Why will an Indian not feel proud of being an Indian if he is allowed to think himself an Indian? There are a few important points like allowing every one to practise his religious faith, fostering a feeling of security of life and property, removing suspicions from others' mind by one's own behaviour, allowing free and fair political activities that are necessary for arousing stronger feelings of Indianness. Religio-cultural freedom, sharing power through free politico-local means, free access to State affairs without any discrimination, providing equal job opportunities and allowing educational facilities to all will go a long way in binding every Indian citizen in the common fabric of Indian national identity.

REFERENCES

Berger, P. and Luckmann. P., *The Social Construction of Reality*, Penguin, 1966.

Jabbi, J.K. "Development of religious identity and prejudice in Sikh children", *Social Change*, 12(4), 20-27, 1981.

Khan, H.R., "A study of the development of religious prejudice in children", in S.N. Singh and H.R. Khan (eds), *Prejudice in Indian Society* (116-133), Varanasi: Rupa Psychological Centre, 1979.

Lauren, K., "Nationellt framlingskap—to narsidentitts problem" (National alienation problem of adolescents identity). *Socialmedicinsk tidskrift*, 6, pp. 359-363, 1973.

Mascovici, S. and Paicheler, G., "Social comparison and recognition" in Tajfel H. (ed),

Differentiation Between Social Groups, Academic Press, 1978.

Naqvi, N., "Relative deprivation and attribution of blame in communal riots". Unpublished doctoral thesis, Allahabad University, Allahabad, 1982.

Prasad, M.B., "Development of caste awareness in children: A theoretical model", *Journal of Social and Economical Studies,* 1, pp. 115-129, 1973.

Reinans, "Invandring? Javisst, men pa vissa villker"! (Immigration? yes, but on certain conditions!) *Ny i Serige,* 1, pp. 37-42.

Sharma, N., *Development of Prejudice in Children,* Bhopal: Well Prints Private Limited, 1986.

Singh, A.K., "Women: The most disliked group ranking of prejudices", *Social Change,* 10(3-4), pp. 3-9, 1980.

Singh, A.K., "The psychology of minority groups in India", *Journal of Social and Economic Studies,* 3, pp. 191-215.

Suri, S. and Husain, M.G., "A study of identity of different ethnic groups: A cross-cultural comparison, *Manas,* 37, 37 (1-2), 1990.

Tajfel, H., "La categorisation social" in Mascovici, S. (ed). *Introduction a la Psychologic Larouse*, Paris, 1972.

Tripathi, R.C. and Srivastava, R., "Relation deprivation and intergroup attitudes", *European Journal of Social Psychology,* 2, pp. 313-318, 1980.

UNESCO, Joint Study Report of the meeting of the international working groups on a joint study of cultural development in countries containing several National or Ethnic Groups. Zegreb, March, 22-24, 1977.

[illegible] *Social Scientist* [illegible]

[illegible] knowledge and the burden of history [illegible] Allen and Unwin [illegible]

Piaget, M. J. [illegible] development [illegible] in children [illegible] Journal [illegible] 1951.

[illegible] on [illegible] (Bombay: [illegible]) [illegible]

[illegible] *Ethnic groups* [illegible] Greenwood Press [illegible]

[illegible] the most disliked ethnic (national) populations [illegible] Vol. [illegible]

[illegible] The psychology of majority-minority [illegible] in India, *Journal of Social and* [illegible] *Studies*, [illegible]

[illegible] and [illegible], M. J., A study of identity of different ethnic groups [illegible] cultural comparison, [illegible] 1990.

[illegible] in [illegible] (ed.) [illegible] 1972.

[illegible] Relation, [illegible] and [illegible] group [illegible] *Journal of Social Psychology*, [illegible] pp. [illegible] 1990.

UNESCO, Joint Study Report of the meeting of the international working groups on a [illegible] study of cultural development in countries containing several national cultures, [illegible] Geneva, March, 1975.

8

DEPRIVED AND NON-DEPRIVED ETHNIC GROUPS – A Study of their Identity

SUSHMA SURI and M.G. HUSAIN

Identity orientation is the result of individual socialization and international aspiration for value and objectives. As a matter of fact the process of self-definition interacts with the development of value system so as to determine the changes in ethnic affiliation and thus people strive for positive social identities.

Identification with a group which represents the negative values of an individual is likely to create identification conflict for him (Weinreich, 1983). It could be said that from birth onwards the child is innately self-willed and self-centred. A child also develops negativism due to the awareness self-will as well as personal distinctiveness. In this way negativism plays an essential role in a child's development of a strong sense of identity. The aim of negativism now is to help the individual to feel distinctive in terms of where he or she stands in relation to a variety of issues. However, if a group is evaluated unfavourably in comparison to a relevant comparison group, a number of reactions are possible, such as individual may respond to threat by reconstructing his or her identity. Secondly, individuals try to activate themselves in order to evade the threat. Thirdly, a new (lower status) out-group may be chosen for comparison (Minard, 1952) in order to avoid threats when centred upon the individual's group membership or individual's group. When a direct attempt is made to change the position of in-group and out-group on the relevant evaluative dimensions, the extent of this competition provides a social conflict. However, the social comparison theory embodies a primary motive to know oneself. That is why one may have drive for "self-evaluation" in addition to a need for self-enhancement through social comparison (Tajfel 1969, 1972; Festinger, 1983). Cofer and Appley (1964) mentioned that there is a general motive to know the environment under social comparison, and in turn many secondary drives emerge such as need for stimulation, affiliation, approval and so on. Maslow (1954) had given the similar viewpoint that a person will aspire for a place in his group and may desire for a stable, firmly based and high evaluation of himself. Thus anything which attacks self-esteem is consequently a serious threat to identity.

However, membership of a particular ethnic group is one of the most important aspects of an individual's identity–how he or she perceives himself or herself and how he or she is perceived by others. The sense of ethnic identity among the majority of an ethnic minority group is very strong and there is little indication that this will simply dissolve in the face of the majority group's way of life. Certain features of the ethnic identity of some minority groups cannot change and they continue to distinguish them from other members of society and thus prevent full assimilation. Thus, common identity is thrust upon those people who are at the receiving end of certain attitudes and identity development is influenced by many factors. These are both internal and external. Individual's values, needs and many other psychological characteristics lead him to identify himself with a particular group or organization. Similarly many social factors like political ideology, religious propaganda, intentionally emotion-arousing situations are also responsible for strengthening of identity. Apart form these factors social and cultural conditions, environmental characteristics, etc., are also decisive forces in identity development.

Quite a large number of studies are available reflecting the fact that deprived people too are very much inclined towards their "own group". This is due to the fact that they live in socially and culturally deprived areas. These places have unorganized structures with improper houses, poor civic facilities, practically no recreational amenities, substandard schools with poor atmosphere for children's education, etc. Because of all these they suffer from emotional disturbances, a feeling of insecurity, frustration, hopelessness and have unsatisfactory attitudes in social relationships. All of these affect their life and they (deprived) maintain themselves independently as groups. This gives rise to alienation from one side and inclination to the other.

The magnitude of deprivation is very high in the case of minorities, i.e. Muslims, Christians, Sikhs and Tribals in India. "Backward" too is used as a synonym of the deprived. Deprivation produces a kind of personality pattern that results in various kinds of inadequacy in behaviour. These changes in self-awareness of the personality assume new capabilities for an objective categorical analysis of one's behaviour. This, in fact, creates new forms of activities. However, their day-to-day problem of survival forces them to develop a feeling of affiliation towards their group. This psychological tie as a matter of fact is their strength identity. The available research carried out in relation to identity shows that identity formation is affected by social as well as psychological factors. Individual's bringing up, interaction with others, his socio-cultural status, etc., influence their identity. Studies also revealed that deprivation leads to stronger identity.

Method and Procedure

The present research is a comparative study of identity of different ethnic groups, i.e. Hindus, Muslims, Sikhs and Scheduled Castes, belonging to two socio-economical backgrounds, viz. deprived and non-deprived. The sample taken for this research consisted of 200 school-going children. All the subjects were within the age bracket of 14-17 years studying in classes IX-XII. Data were collected in the Union Territory of Delhi. In order to get information regarding their deprivation level and identity a scale, namely, 'deprivation, identity and socio-cultural status scale', developed by Husain (1985) was administered to all the subjects. All the obtained scores of this factorial designed study, i.e. ethnic groups (4) and socio-economic status (2), were analysed with the help of X: Percentages of scores on different dimensions of identity of all the groups were also obtained to show the trend of results.

Results and Discussion

Tables 1 to 4 show the results obtained with the help of X and percentages.

TABLE 1: National Identity

	A	B	C	D	X^2
Deprived	20.08	13.94	8.64	20.36	0.19*
Non-deprived	22.80	12.60	9.28	21.28	

TABLE 2: Religious Identity

	A	B	C	D	X^2
Deprived	60.76	90.80	95.43	61.46	10.31**
Non-deprived	50.00	70.52	78.52	53.52	

TABLE 3: Cultural Identity

	A	B	C	D	X^2
Deprived	32.00	40.16	41.83	39.08	10.1**
Non-deprived	27.88	31.56	32.48	30.00	

TABLE 4: Linguistic Identity

	A	B	C	D	X^2
Deprived	38.52	46.44	45.88	40.88	123**
Non-deprived	32.16	39.12	37.24	38.32	

* Insignificant
** Significant at .01 level
A = Hindu, B = Muslim, C = Sikh D = Scheduled Caste

The results obtained by using X and percentages showed that the deprived groups have a salient religious, cultural and linguistic identity as followed by their non-deprived counterparts. On the other hand, all the groups belonging to both deprived and non-deprived environmental conditions showed similar national identity scores. To be more specific there was no significant difference among different groups (X^2 = .19). It is perhaps more reasonable to explain that greater differences are simply due to a larger availability of social identity categories. Scheduled Caste subjects had a very high national identity. This is because of the fact that the Scheduled Caste are the most deprived segment in Indian society with regard to culture, economic conditions and social status. They have strongly identified with Indian nationality. This is just because of their low socio-economic and disadvantaged cultural background, i.e. extent of deprivation. This assertiveness towards their religion, culture, and language and nationality, shows that different ethnic groups define their personal rejection and dissociation. These groups in India did not show any stronger sign of life in harmony with one another (ethnic groups).

Our results get support from the findings of Hutnik (1984) and Husain(1985). On the basis of their studies they reported that British subjects showed a higher national self-consciousness than their Indian and West Indian counterparts. However, social conflict breeds social identity and social identity breeds social conflicts. These social identities are ethnicized. Deprived subjects of this study irrespective of ethnicity and religion have shown a stronger identity as compared to their non-deprived counterparts. This might also be because of discrimination they face and their strong will to survive. This study further supports the findings of Kunje (1985) who said that cultural awareness increases identity among ethnic minorities. Deprived subjects are not only deprived in terms of physical and material circumstances and surroundings but are also deprived of psychological values like respect and acceptance in society. Lack of all these facilities makes such subjects feel deprived in their own terms, and even in this different and difficult situation they want to survive. As a result they maintain allegiance towards their religion, culture, language, group, etc. It is also believed on the basis of a large number of studies that there is a strong connection between the environment and the behaviour of an individual. Lewin's (1935) emphasis that the close interconnection and isomorphism between a person and the situation is also in line with our findings. Our results are also in conformity with the results of Kincaid (1975) who believed that deprived subjects pose more serious adjustment problems.

In order to lessen the ethnic conflict this becomes more important to observe the causes of aggression and assertion of these identities both in historical perspective as well as in today's context. The option of having a separate group identity assimilates the groups into the State but not into the nation and consequently the deprived groups remain permanently deprived. Therefore, in order to lessen the communal conflict, the deprived should understand the proper notion of their identity. It should not be much separative to make them aliens in their own homeland and should not be so diffused as to lose its distinctiveness. Another important concern with the ethnic divides is to subsume other ethnic identities and develop Indian national identity among all the Indian citizens. The Indian national identity need not clash with other ethnic sub-identities. Loyalty towards their nation is the most important factor in removing or minimizing ethnic conflicts. National identity must be stronger than other sub-national identities. Religion, caste, ethnicity, language and culture alone do not provide the basis for the commonness. The component of the Indian national identity must be acceptable to all Indians. One of the important facts to understand is that diversity should not be stretched to the point of separativeness. Similarly, integration should not be stretched to the point of complete assimilation and loss of distinctive identity as a such group within the nation. Here, in this case, one has to try to achieve a delicate balance as an important and vital goal of the process of nation-building. All the sects of the society, including the deprived, should have proper access to participation in social and national affairs without any discrimination.

REFERENCES

Adams, A.A., "The effect of planned background on economically disadvantaged Kindergarten children", (unpublished doctoral thesis), Mississippi State University, 1971.

Carrington, B., "Sport as a side-track. An analysis of West Indian involvement in extracurricular sport", in L. Barton and S. Walker (eds), *Race, Class and Education*, London: Croom Helm, 1983.

Cashmore, E. Black, Sportsman, London: Routledge and Kegan Paul. Cofer, C. N. and Appley, M.H., *Motivation: Theory and Research*, Wiley: New York, 1964.

De Board, Low, "The achievement syndrome among Negro and White culturally disadvantaged body (unpublished doctoral thesis), Vanderbit University, 1969.

Kincaid, J.C., *Poverty and Equality in Britain: A Study of Social Security and Taxation*, Penguin Books, 1975.

Lewin, K., *A Dynamic Theory of Psychology*, N.Y.: McGraw-Hill, 1935.

Maslow, A.H., *Motivation and Personality*, Harper: New York, 1954.

McCoy, M.M., "A reconstruction of emotion", in Bannister, D. (ed), *Academic Psyciat*, 27, pp. 277-288, 1977.

Minard, R.D., "Race relationship in the Pocahonts coalfields" *Journal of Social Issues*, 25, pp. 29-44, 1952.

Tajfel, H., "Cognitive aspects of prejudice", *Journal of Social Issues*, 25, pp. 79-97, 1969.

Tajfel, H., "La categorisation socialin", Mascovici, S. (ed), *Introduction a la Psychologic Larouse*, Paris, 1972.

Tajfel, H. and Turner, J.C., "An interrogative theory of intergroup conflict", in W.G. Austin and S. Wocchel (eds), *The Social Psychology of Intergroup Relation*, Book Cole: Monterey, California, 1979.

Weinreich, P., "A conceptual framework for exploring identity development: Identity Structure Analysis and Index", *10th International Congress of the International Association for Child and Adolescent Psychiatry and Allied Professions*, Trinity.

9

DEMOCRACY AND NATIONAL INTEGRATION:
Political Rationalities

PETER RONALD D'SOUZA

The codeword, figuratively and historically, for the struggle underway in India is *Maha-Bharat.* Not only is it a struggle between "good" and "evil" although the perspectives on these terms are many, but it is also a struggle for the soul of modern India, for that distinctiveness of mind and philosophy, practice and construct, which give to a people and their place an identity and which make them a nation. The struggle is at base a struggle of definition and design over the substantive nature and content of the populist slogan "unity in diversity".

Although there are many variants to this slogan, for purposes of clarity, however, two poles will be identified: the one represented by the Congress of Nehru[1] where the emphasis is on the recognition and protection of diversity within the unity of the nation, the theme here being an existence of cultural plurality, and the other represented by the BJP where the focus is on unity, the roots of which lie in a culture that is rich and ancient and distinctive, and one where the diversities are and should be subsumed within the unity.[2] The argument in the latter case is for seeing the plurality of community and ethnicity merely as subcultural forms within the mainstream of *Hindutva.*[3] These two armies of ideas, beliefs, attitudes, practices and responses, are in struggle on the plains of India today. The more specific concern with "national integration", therefore, gains relevance within this larger attempt at setting out the terms of the relationship between the parts and the whole, terms that determine the nature of the institutional design made up of rights, obligations, procedures for distribution of social resources, restrictions, opportunities, etc.

The issue of national integration itself needs to be disaggregated into its normative and empirical components, where the questions in the former case relate to what should be the nature of the institutional design, and in the latter case what are the factors that prevent or promote the realization of the design. The normative level sets the ethical parameters for the configuration of institutions that make up, and are to make up, the Indian State. At this normative level is the struggle of the two visions referred to above where a "secular" India based on the coexistence and protection of a plurality of cultures is in contest with a "secular" India based on the subsumption of subcultures within a larger culture. At the empirical level, in contrast, are the social and historical processes that input into the making of the nation such as an emotional commitment to the idea of nationhood, an economic interest that sets alternatives and opportunities, a political rationality that unfolds in an unmanageable direction and at an unmanageable pace, a religious world that influences the interaction between segments, etc. It is the play and interplay of these different domains, with their different internal and external logics, that determine the probability of success of either vision. In both camps democracy is regarded as the instrumentality for promoting the objectives. This brief paper is an attempt at posing some inconvenient questions to arguments at both levels especially in the context of a multi-ethnic, multi-linguistic, multi-religious, and multi-racial society such as that of India where the institutions and processes of democracy have taken root.

At the outset, however, two comments are in order about the term "national integration" itself. The first is that it is not merely just a descriptive term as suggested by some of the earlier literature on "political modernization".[4] This can be established by the argument that the term "integration", in common parlance, has itself become a value word, i.e. integration is always preferable to disintegration. When it is, however, coupled with the word "national" the commendatory connotation loses its universal appeal and in some cases gives rise to its opposite, a condemnatory connotation. This occurs because of the varying experience of the "nation" that various groups may have had, beneficial in one case, oppressive in the other. An inquiry into the responses to the word "nation" itself would reveal a great deal about the history of the relationship between the parts and the whole, between the smaller ethnic and religious communities and the large collectivity, the nation. Responses are, after all, carriers of a complex process of socialization. The term "national integration" is, therefore, both evaluative and explanatory.

The other comment concerns what may appear to be a somewhat unrelated issue but which, I wish to argue, is present at the level of hidden assumptions in any debate on national integration. The assumption behind a statement on "national integration" is that there are objective "interests" common to all the parts that are integrating and that once such an integration has taken place it will result in a recognition by the parts of these common interests. This is a variant of the Hegelian conception of historical evolution. In other words the argument for national integration implies the possibility of subjective and objective consensus on the basic issues of the structure and substance of the nation. This hidden assumption gains significance, for the study of developing societies today, because this belief in the possibility of societal level "consensus" on major issues of political principle, i.e., on the institutional design of a polity, was the basis of a major controversy in the debate on democracy in the 50s and 60s[5], and although dormant for a decade and a half, has re-emerged in the late 80s as a result of the changes taking place in the erstwhile socialist countries. The most challenging exponents of this argument are J.K. Galbraith,[6] and Daniel Bell.[7] Some Indian scholarship too has come to endorse a weaker version of this thesis.[8] I have drawn attention to this hidden assumption, of the possibility of a consensus on institutional design, (i) because arguments for national integration appear to imply this, (ii) because theorists concerned with models for change have begun to re-assert the argument that these models can only be variants of the liberal-democratic model, and (iii) because theorists of political development have begun to prescribe strategies for developing countries whereby a possible legal and/or moral agreement on fundamentals, a consensus, is seen as the best strategy for consolidating democracy in these countries.

In such circumstances, the consolidation of democracy – so intimately linked to structural economic reform – requires the negotiation of some kind of agreement of "pact" among competing political parties and social forces on: (1) the braod direction and principles of structural economic reform, which all parties will support, no matter which one's come to power; (2) a renunciation of certain political appeals and strategies – in particular an irresponsible but tempting politics of outbidding; (3) sacrifices that all social forces will share, including demands they will mutually postpone during the initial and highly unstable period of economic adjustment and democratic installation; and (4) a method of ensuring that the burdens of adjustment are shared more or less fairly and eased by relief measures for the hardest-hit groups such as workers rendered jobless by structural reforms.[9]

The preceding preliminary remarks are intended (i) to expose the value-slope behind the arguments on national integration; (ii) to caution against a form of "scientism" which the suggestion of consensus can slide into, a paradigm of argument which suggests that all political problems can be resolved "technically" since consensus on major issues has been achieved.[10] The central belief in politics being the terrain where solutions to social problems can be worked out gets substituted by the belief in technology being the domain where these solutions can be found. Nehru belonged to an intellectual tradition which placed inordinately high faith in technological solutions. The persistence of problems that technology was supposed to address, their change of form and their appearance at a different level of struggle, however, only emphasizes the centrality of the political terrain, the importance of democracy as the political form best suited for resolving these problems. The preceding remarks were also intended (iii) to distinguish between two types of investigations on "national integration" the empirical and normative and, the most pertinently (iv) to highlight the struggle between competing visions of what should be the substance and parameters of such national integration.

Although some of the more fundamental issues are being argued out within and between these two visions,[11] this paper will not attempt to adjudicate between the two but instead confront either with consequences which necessarily emerge because of the initial choice of democracy. It will attempt to show that the historical project of democracy in modern India, which began with the Indian National Movement, has set into motion certain rationalities, at both the attitudinal and organizational levels, which in the short term, particularly, come into conflict with the task of "national integration", howsoever defined. Over time these conflicts may weaken or grow in intensity, the direction eventually taken being dependent upon the processes of democracy, seen as that political formation which is both the means to the solution and the solution itself.

The idea of democracy basically rests on the assumption and assertion of the equality of all human beings qua human beings. This manifests itself in three ways: (i) by recognizing an equal claim by all to equal respect for their persons and their interests, i.e., moral equality, (ii) by endorsing the equal right of adult persons to determine for themselves what their goals and values are to be and what is in their own interests, i.e., personal autonomy, and (iii) by guaranteeing the equal capacity to determine or influence collective decisions, i.e., political equality.[12] The acceptance of democracy is the acceptance, even at a minimal level, of political institutions that safeguard and promote these aspects of equality. When we in India accepted this idea of equality at the political level when we gave ourselves a constitution, then we set into motion a conflict of rationalities between what Geertz called the "old society" and the "new state".[13] The old society constituted around patterns of inequality[14] is in tension and conflict with the new State constituted around patterns of equality. These patterns, compelled to occupy the same geographical and historical space, begin to compete for the social, political and economic spaces as well. It is a long-drawn-out competition, with occasional pauses and frequent clashes (e.g. Mandal, with insidious encroachements, e.g. public interest litigation, and overt manoeuvrings, e.g., the Narmada Project). In this struggle equality is able to push back inequality from some aspects of the traditional terrain, such as the social practices of purity and pollution. In its early expression the demand for equality takes the form of a demand for equality of political rights, which then grows into a demand for equality of economic results.[15]

Identities and the Struggle for Dominance

There is, however, no final battle between equality and inequality, only strategic retreats, changes in form as when status shifts from caste to class, and historically expedient compromises of limited longevity, e.g., voting for the Congress Party in 1984 because the nation was considered in danger. This equilibrium, sometimes achieved, is always temporary as the old perspectives have become exhausted and the new perspectives have still to assert themselves. The point to be noted, however, is that the acceptance of democracy puts the demand for equality, in its many manifestations, squarely on the political agenda. This gives rise to new political realities with their concomitant new political identities. It is these identities, and the struggle for dominance of each, that we are witnessing in India today.

This struggle between patterns of equality and patterns of inequality has built into it a commitment to participation by citizens in the affairs of the polity. Theoretically this participation has three aspects:

(i) equal *freedom* of participation where the thrust is on the freedom of vote, expression and association, (ii) equal *opportunity* of participation where the preoccupation is with the capacity to perceive political alternative and the availability of preferred alternatives, and (iii) equal *participation* where the concern is with issues such as voting equality, majority principle, etc.[16]

This participation, in practice, may be somewhere in the range between limited and extended participation but in India this still represents an advance over the political participation available before the achievement of universal franchise. The introduction of participation even of the limited form of voting, has a dramatic effect on the enfranchised citizen. The act of participation creates a consciousness of interest and of rights which has its own rationality and develops its own momentum. Participation becomes the vehicle by which the parts, i.e., groups within the polity, make demands on the whole, i.e. the State.

Political participation is seen by democratic theorists as having both a protective and a developmental role. The protective argument sees participation as the best way to promote one's interests and rights (J.S. Mill) and to protect them from tyranny (Madison). Political participation is advocated because of a distrust of those in positions of power and because of the belief that only those governments which allow such participation are legitimate. The developmental argument sees it as an activity by which members of a polity acquire citizenship, gain a sense of involvement in the system and develop a feeling of responsibility towards others and towards the State (Tocqueville). Political participation develops in the participant a sense of proportion about one's interests and rights, about the demands one can and should make on the State.[17] This sense of proportion, however, evolves through a series of struggles with "others" and with "oneself" and it is these struggles which either forge the larger community, the nation, through negotiation and compromise between groups, or destroy it when such compromises cannot be struck. It is with regard to this process, where a consciousness of rights develops and where this consciousness gets subsequently articulated as political activity, that there is disagreement between theorists of political development over the mode, quality and intensity of political participation that should be allowed in a developing society, e.g., India.[18]

Extended democracy in a developing society, it is held, leads to contradiction between (a) conflict and consensus, (b) representativeness and governability, and (c) consent and effectiveness.[19] These contradictions do appear because, as I have stated earlier, of the project of equality expressing itself through the participatory mode. The question that theorists of democracy and national integration must consider is whether the appropriate response to these contradictions is "less democracy" (as suggested by developmental theorists such as Larry Diamond)[20] or "more democracy" (as suggested by radicals such as Randhir Singh).[21]

The project of equality generates these contradictions because the project site is a highly inegalitarian, plural society. India is today probably the most complex plural polity in the world. Not only is there a plurality of groups but also a plurality of identities within each individual. I am, for example, a Goan, a Konkani speaker, a member of a minority group, a South Indian, a member of the educated elite, etc. These multiple identities in a democracy get activated by those processes that are concerned with establishing the terms that are to govern the relationship between the parts and the whole, terms that determine the manner in which social resources are to be distributed. Contradictions and conflicts are a result of the attempt by the different identities to determine the substance of these terms. They take many forms.

> Ethnic affinity in India is expressed in terms of various identifying groupings such as religion, language, region, or caste. . . . Indians are multi-ethnic both in terms of plural social division and multiple personal identification. This multiplicity leads to a perplexing series of cross-closures for bargaining, rivalry and combination that are quite different from the mutually reinforcing ethnic ties.[22]

These tensions are, therefore, an inevitable consequence of the acceptance of democracy. They are not deviations or pathologies but expressions of the democratizing process.[23] We must see them, therefore, both with a sense of history, i.e., as the result of a process of social transformation and a sense of politics, i.e., the recognition that the remedies are political. As the English political pluralists J.N. Figgis and Harold Laski have argued, not only do such groups exist but ought to exist in a healthy state since they constitute and ought to constitute the principal bulwark against State absolutism. The question these English pluralists asked was not "how much uniformity is to be imposed but instead how much diversity is to be allowed and encouraged without threatening the unity of the State".[24] In a plural society when the goal of equality, embodied in the project of democracy, finds expression through the participatory mode, conflicts and cleavages will necessarily emerge. In an old society these conflicting groups will take an ethnic form.

> The ideal model of a democratic society was a centripetal society. The reality is a centrifugal society, which has not just one centre of power (the "general will" envisaged by Rousseau) but a plethora of them, and which deserves the name... of polycentric society or polyarchy.[25]

What Theorists of National Integration Must Do?

Theorists of national integration must, therefore, not just recognize the existence of a plural society but must also design the institutions to allow the plurality to grow. In the Indian context, especially today, after about forty years of universal franchise, the institutions and procedures of demand processing and conflict resolution seem inadequate to the task, an inadequacy due to many factors from inherently faulty design, i.e., the institutions were not planned for the magnitude of demand that emerged, to a subversion of their initial purpose, i.e., the means to an end becoming an end-in-itself, to a manipulation of their functioning, i.e., the control by dominant caste and class groups over policy making and policy implementation.

In India pluralism as an ancient feature of the social fabric has, as a result of democracy, begun to take on the features of a pluralism of political organizations. To give full expression to this inherent pluralism of the social fabric, however, more organizations are required, not just in the realm of economy but in that of society and culture as well. At the level of design it is unclear whether this requires a new federalism to be negotiated especially since democracy has released aspirations which the old framework seems unable to address. This would mean a change in the terms of the relationship between the Centre and the States, between States and Regions and between Regions and Localities. Within the "unity in diversity" theme this may imply more fiscal and political decentralization in terms of both the institutions that make up the State and also in terms of the other organizations of the polity.

To the key concepts of equality, participation and plurality, used to explore the issue of democracy and national integration so far, two more need to be added to balance the analysis, the concepts of competition and of power. Although the concept of competition has largely been associated only with the liberal democratic model, especially after J.A. Schumpeter's (1942) book *Capitalism, Socialism and Democracy*[26] it has today especially after the transformations in the erstwhile socialist bloc in Europe, come to be regarded as central to democratic discourse itself.[27] Competition between leaders and between groups is seen as the process by which interests are protected and political leaders made accountable.[28] While competition may exacerbate conflict and cleavage, since success in the competition enables the successful to set the terms by which resources will be distributed, it may, after a historical period of heightened competition, produce more tolerance and less conflict, more support for procedures of interest adjudication and less hostility to opposing groups, more open institution and more legitimate State. While no general rule can be formulated about the consequences of competition, the above are likely to occur as long as adequate institutions are also created to handle this increased competition. The conflicts and hostility that we see in India today, which are the result of the processes of competitive democratic politics and which threaten the very stability of the State itself, are able to do so because the competition is between unequals, because the conditions of equality mentioned above are not satisfied.

In a society such as India the competitive requirements of democratic politics are double-edged in that, on the one hand, it becomes the method by which a certain openness, efficiency, accountability and protection of individual and group interest becomes possible while, on the other hand, it becomes the process by which politically dormant social identities become active, populism becomes endemic through the "politics of outbidden", construction of the identity of the "other" becomes exclusionary and of the "self" purist, and the potential for violent strife such as, communal conflict, grows.

The final concept through which the "unity in diversity" theme should be analysed is the concept of power. Power in its various manifestations permeates all structures of society. Power here refers to an asymmetrical relationship between at least two entities whereby one of the entities, because of this asymmetry, is able to bring about desired consequences. The preceding discussion of equality, participation, pluralism and competition gets a "three-dimensional"[29] perspective only when viewed in terms of the power structures between individuals, groups, classes and regions. This asymmetry diminishes the quality and more of participation and renders democratic competition as competition between unequals. The project of democracy is, therefore, an unfinished project since it is about redesigning these power structures of society along egalitarian lines. It is here where the future agenda of national integration must be located where the *Maha-Bharat* is to be fought.

NOTES

1. Kaviraj, S. 1989. "Ironies of History", *Seminar,* 363, pp. 432-48.
2. Thapar, R. 1991. "Religion, Culture and Nation", *Seminar*, 377.
3. Dubashi, J. 1990. *Independent,* October 30, 1990. He writes "...we Hindus have become a timid race, almost a cowardly race. We lack the courage of our convictions. Some of us don't even have convictions, and have been trying to hide our shame under high-sounding but empty phrases like 'secularism'. For the last so many centuries, the history of the Hindus has been created by non-Hindus, first the Moghuls, then the British. Even today the Hindus are being denied their right to write their own history, which to me is like genocide. Until we write our own history this land cannot be ours... the whole purpose of the Ayodhya movement is to change the history of India, nothing less, nothing more...."
   "For the first time in several centuries, the history of India is being made by Indian, call them Hindu, call them anything, else if the word Hindu sticks in your gullet as it did Nehru's ... freedom does not mean flying your own flag or having your own government. Freedom means making your own history, writing it in your own blood in the pages of time..... We Hindus were not born yesterday. We were not born in the British Museum and did not emerge from the dog-eared copies of ancient history books. We are history personified. History with a capital H....."
4. Weiner, M. 1971. "Political Integration and Political Development", in Claude, E. Welch (Jr), *Political Modernization: A Reader in comparative Political Change,* California: Wadesworth Pub. Co., pp. 180-196.
5. Kariel, H (ed.). 1970. *Frontiers of Democratic Theory,* Random House, New York.
6. Galbraith, J.K. 1989. "Convergence and Post-History", in *New Perspective Quarterly,* Fall, pp. 46-52.
7. Bell, D. 1988. "The End of Ideology Revisited", in *Government and Opposition,* Vol. 23, No. 2/3, pp. 131-150 & 321-331.
8. Datta-Chaudhari, M. 1991. "Mandal and the Berlin Wall", *Seminar,* 377.
9. Diamond, L. 1990. "Three paradoxes of Democracy", in *Journal of Democracy,* Vol. 1, No 3, pp. 48-60. The economic consensus in summary form is that market economies develop while socialist economies fall behind!
10. Keat, R. 1981. *The Politics of Social Theory,* University of Chicago Press: Chicago.
11. Kaviraj, S. "Why do we lack common sense?" Sabherwal, S. "On the Social Crises of India: Political Traditions", *Occasional Papers on History and Society,*

Nehru Memorial Museum and Library, No. vii; Kumar, R. "India: A Nation-State or Civilization-State," *Occasional Papers on Perspectives in Indian Development,* Nehru Memorial Museum and Library, No. viii.

12. Lively, J. 1990. "In the Centrifugal System", *Times Literary Supplement,* January 5-11.
13. Geertz, C. (ed). 1963. *Old Societies and New States,* Amerind: New Delhi.
14. Beteille, A. 1977. *Inequality among Men*, Basil Blackwell: Delhi.
15. Berlin, I. 1977. "Equality", in *Concepts and Categories,* Oxford University Press: Oxford.
16. Oppenheim F. 1971. "Democracy: Characteristics included and excluded", *The Monist,* 55. pp. 29-50.
17. Keim, D.W. 1975. "Participation in Contemporary Democratic Theories", in Pennock, J.R. and J. Chapman (eds), *Participation in Politics,* New York: Lieber-Atherton.
18. Diamond, L., J. Linz; S.M. Lipset (eds), *Democracy in Asia,* Vistaar Publications: New Delhi.
19. Diamond, L. 1990. "Three Paradoxes of Democracy", in *Journal of Democracy,* Vol. 1, No. 3, pp. 48-60: Weiner, M. *The Indian Paradox: Essays in Indian Politics,* Sage: New Delhi.
20. *Ibid.*
21. This solution was given by Singh at a lecture on "Communalism in India", in Panaji, organized by the *Goa Association for Political Science*, on February 21, 1991.
22. Das Gupta, J. 1988. "Ethnicity, Democracy and Development in India: Assam in a General Perspective", in Atul Kohli (ed), *India's Democracy,* Princeton University Press: N.J.
23. Dahl, R. 1986. "Polyarchy, Pluralism and Scale", in *Democracy, Liberty and Equality,* Norwegian University Press: Oslo.
24. Nicholls, D. 1974. *Three Varieties of Pluralism,* Macmillan: London.
25. Bobbio, N. 1987. *The Future of Democracy,* Tr. R. Griffin, ed. R. Bellamy, Polity Press: Cambridge, p-28.
26. Macpherson, C.B. 1973. *Democratic Theory: Essay in Retrieval,* Clarendon Press: Oxford.
27. Miller, D. 1989. *Market, State and Community,* Clarendon Press: Oxford.
28. The debate on democracy should not be whether competition is desirable or not, but rather what other processes, in addition to competition between leaders and between groups, need to be developed to extend democracy in any society.
29. Lukes, S. 1979. *Power: A Radical View,* London: Macmillan.

10

TO GOVERN OR NOT TO GOVERN?: Dilemma of the New Indian Party System

MAHENDRA PRASAD SINGH

In the politics of a country of India's size and diversity, a crucial question is the one that relates to the overarching framework of *political aggregation* and governance. *A central ideological State apparatus*[1] *straddling the civil society and the State* that performs this *crucial function* in modern political systems is *the party system.* In the early post-independence decades the predominant "*Congress system*" –with its internal Census in close democratic interaction with marginal Opposition parties of pressure–footed this bill (Rajni Kothari, 1970, Ch.5). Still later, what came to pass was a new system of Congress system in that it lacked the internal party pluralism of the Nehru era and was centrally controlled by Indira Gandhi, whose administration subsequently also came under increasing pressures of extra-parliamentary mass movements, Opposition parties, and federal and judicial organs of the State (Myron Weiner, 1989, Ch.3).

With the precipitous electoral decline of the Congress in the late 1980s, India faces the prospects of a fractionalized multi-party system in which the major contenders for national power appear to be the following: (1) Congress, still the largest and most extensive party; (2) Janata Dal, the next largest party in 1989 but suffering a major split at year-end; (3) Bhartiya Janata Party that shot up to the third position in the 1989 parliamentary elections riding on tides of Hindu revivalism; and (4) Communist parties that have registered a steady rise in their vote-share and parliamentary representation over the years. All of these are national parties and each controls–singly or in coalition–more than one State Government. To these, we must add the Janata Dal (Samajwadi) that split off from the Janata Dal and formed a minority government of the centre with Congress support in mid-

November, 1990, and "controlled some State Governments as well. . . . Its formation followed the fall of the Janata Dal led minority government of the National Front installed in November, 1989".[2] Moreover, the picture is also complicated by an assortment of regional parties, e.g. Akali Dals, National Conference, Dravida Munnetra Kazhagams (All India Anna, and Anna), Telugu Desam, Asom Gana Parished, to name only the major ones.[3] Broadly, these are, then, the major elements of India's new party system ushered in by the 1989 parliamentary elections. The new party system broadly conforms to the model of "polarized pluralism" offered in Giovanni Sartori's (1976) typology of comparative party systems.

In the early decades of independence the main challenges to the new constitutional regime had come from communist and tribal insurgencies. In the current phase, these challenges come from religious and linguistic nationalities in the country and its neighbourhood. Among earlier achievements of democratic national integration and constitutionalization of political forces involving communists, communalists, Tamilian parties, and North East tribals, there are new twists and turns that put question marks on past records. *New reversals* in the case of religious communalist forces are particularly recurrent causing deepest anxieties. The Akali Dals and National Conference in the past decade have become marginalized by militant secessionist movements in Punjab and Jammu and Kashmir. Both these parties have often also shown ambivalence to religious fundamentalism or secessionism, Centrist parties have failed to resist the lure of covert communal and caste mobilization. The BJP has gone back to its roots in Hindu communalism turning its back to an earlier phase of liberalization and secularization. The ambivalence of the AGP and DMK governments towards the activities of the United Liberation Front of Assam and the Liberation Tigers of Tamil Eelam have recently incurred the wrath of the Janata Party (Samajwadi) minority government in New Delhi and its allies (Congress and AIADMK); both these State Governments have been sacked under Article 356 of the Constitution providing for imposition of President's rule in a State.

The major all-India parties – Congress and Janata Dal – themselves have been in ferment. The Janata Dal was first rocked by factionalism during its eleven-month rule at the head of the National Front Government between its Jan Morcha and Lok Dal constituents, and subsequently it got embroiled in the new reservation controversies kicked off by the National Front Government's decision in August,

1990, to reserve 27 per cent Central Government and public sector jobs for the Other Backward Classes, in addition to the prevailing 22.5 per cent for the Scheduled Castes/Tribes. Finally, the Janata Dal-led National Front Government was ditched by the BJP when the latter's triumphant Hindu-revivalist and communalist *Rath Yatra* from Somnath to Ayodhya was brought to a halt in Samastipur (Bihar) by the Bihar Government's decision to arrest Mr. L.K. Advani, BJP president. The National Front Government fell on November 7, 1990 in a no-trust vote in Parliament.

The Congress Party itself has gone through factional tussles, changing its Chief Ministers in the wake of communal riots during the pendency of a mandate in Andhra Pradesh, Karnataka and Maharashtra. Recent Congress factionalism in States displays a new dimension in place of the earlier pattern of "horizontal" factionalism between State-level party elements quarrelling and central party leadership arbitrating, the recent factional fights have become "vertical", itself into the vortex. But the party has somchow managed to hold on to its forts in Andhra and Karnataka, with the authority of its national leader Rajiv Gandhi remaining intact.

The minority governments formed in quick succession since the November 1989 parliamentary elections have managed to skate on a very *thin ice of an ambiguous national consensus which is very limited, given the wide divergence of perspectives and electoral ambitions of the major parties.* The agricultural and industrial policies of these governments have been in a state of flux on account of internal differences within the parties supporting these governments from outside, to say nothing of the parties formally in the Opposition. The *reluctance of the alliance parties* of the Governments to formally *join them in a governing coalition,* or at least *to hammer out a common minimum programme before committing their support to the governments, has created an unpredictable political situation.* This has encouraged an *attitude of uncommitment on the part of both the Government and the Opposition* and a *spirit of adventurism* and back-stabbing. It is in this light that one can make sense of the spectacles of V.P. Singh unilaterally announcing the new reservation policy for OBCs and plunging the country into the throes of a caste war. Or of the BJP posing a direct challenge to the secular character of the Indian State by undertaking Advani's *Rath Yatra* in defiance of the very NF Government that it was pledged to support on the floor of Parliament. These acts do not make a parliamentary sense. If anything, Congress and

Communist records of supporting these governments are better, even though they, too, cannot escape the charge of seeking to enjoy power without responsibility. Conversely, the governments have made themselves open to the criticism of coming to power *anyhow,* even at the cost of eating the humble pie of responsibility without power.

Paralysis of the Will to Govern

The Indian party system since the 1989 parliamentary elections has been afflicted with a paralysis of the will to govern. Thus ungovernability is evident on two planes. While the mass electorate has mandated a multi-party system with polarized pluralism (albeit fraught with sociological and ideological contradictions), the party system elites, particularly those belonging to the major centrist parties, have not become attuned to the new political realities. *They still have the hang-ups of the predominant party mentality actually enjoyed in the past or imagined or aspired for the future.* Another face of the ungovernability marking the party system may be seen in the marginalization of the normal institutional processes of politics in some States or parts thereof due to ethnic fundamentalism, class radicalism and Naxalite violence, as also growing criminalization of politics, political and administrative corruption, and electoral violence.

The plain fact of the matter is that *Indian politics is fast becoming some sort of a medieval fort-holding operation between warring caudillos:* the *governmental forces are swarmed by extra-parliamentary mass movements and internal parliamentary disorders* by the Opposition almost instantly after an electoral mandate. There is no patience, either on the part of the Government or the Opposition, to respect the authenticity of the mandate to rule given by the voter to a Parliament or State legislature. Unbending postures adopted by governments even in defiance of persistent and legitimate demands of parliamentary oppositions leads to cynicism and tendency to take to the streets. Having tasted the tumult and might disharmonies of plebiscitary mass mobilizations, the Opposition gets addicted to it and never wants to return to the mundane task of rational parliamentary debates and ventilation of grievances. The one feeds on the other, creating a vicious circle.

A fresh poll has led to the election of a multi-partisan parliament, with the Congress Party as the largest, but not a majority party, a stable pattern of governance still remains dependent on the support of the opposition parties. (Either for ideological incompatibilities or for the lingering hope of returning to power with a predominant party status, the major parties show a barely concealed contempt for rubbing shoulders with smaller parliamentary parties in a coalition government). This leads to half-hearted attempts of back-seat driving by lending parliamentary support to minority governments. The only saving grace has been that all this has not resulted in the unsavoury politics of defection that characterized legislative politics in North Indian States in the late 1960s and early 1970s.[5] But a realignment of political forces on the parliamentary floor in November, 1990, did lead to the piquant situation in which the Lok Sabha Speaker, Mr. Rabi Ray, and the Delhi High Court were called upon to separate Janata Dal dissenters from defectors under the provisions of the Anti-Defection Act (1985) enshrined in the Tenth Schedule of the Constitution.[6]

Politics not for the Uncommitted

The mass circulation print media in India is perhaps the most developed Fourth Estate in the Third World. It is privately owned and it balances the overt and bland pro-government stance of the electronic mass media, until recently under direct government control but now made into a corporation under the Prasar Bharati Act (1990). Not only the Doordarshan (TV) but also the Press have fallen victim to their perverse narcissistic self-image of the larger-than-life builders of mass opinions. The Press, in particular, has in recent years been wont to take a perverse pleasure in demonstrating its unpurposive power. In the morning it unwittingly sets up one straw-man or the other as a Nietzschean hero only to demolish it later in the day with an equal or even greater vengeance. The script of a similar media play has been going on in Tamil Nadu state politics where the popular Tamil film media has been politically hijacked by the rival DMK parties. And the Telugu, Kannada and Hindi cinema have also rushed to join the game with varying measures of success. In a traditional society it is likely for leaders to be carried away by revolutionary designs of political transformation. But there has to be an appropriate blend of strategies of governance and those of transformation in democracy. *Otherwise, why not play the role of revolutionary in the first place.* Both democratic and revolutionary transformations are serious commitments. Politics is not for the uncommitted.

In any case, what we have been witnessing in the post-Nehru India is neither a true variant of the Westminster majoritarian model nor one of the consensus models of democracy.[7] It is fast degenerating into an Indianized version of a caudillo democracy in which money and muscle power, on the one hand, and the coercive State apparatus, on the other, are increasingly allowed and called upon to encroach on and vitiate the channels of institutional politics. A way out of the current impasse lies, besides in democratic reforms, in political elites' realization that coalition governments are not inherently unstable or ineffective, as is clearly demonstrated by Scandinavian, West German and, to an extent, Canadian experiments. President R. Venkataraman, in his 1991 Republic Day broadcast to the nation aptly defended the coalition idea, asserting that it was really "an outmoded political vocabulary that describes the post-1990 Lok Sabha as a 'hung' parliament".[8] It is amazing that none among the political actors has made a plea for giving a coalition government a chance. Instead, they have all chased the ideas of an all-party national government (V.P. Singh, Atal Behari Vajpayee, Devi Lal) and a switch-over to a presidential form of government (Vasant Sathe, L.K. Advani).[9] These diagnoses apparently spring from perceptions of a nation in a deep crisis complicated further by the spectre of governmental instability. But a national government can at best be an emergency measure, and presidentialism is neither the only nor the most suitable way of ensuring governmental stability in India.

It is remarkable that India was in 1990-91 practically without a government willing or able to govern for more than a year. And all this in the midst of grave dangers of secessionism and terrorism within and around. If in the midst of all this, India has not fallen apart it is mainly because of a minimally compensating role of its Administrative State, largely a creation of the British colonial and post-colonial ruling elites.[10]

I believe what we really need as a long-term measure is to create multiple mechanisms for generating consensus in our deeply divided society. The socio-cultural diversities of India were anticipated to be too strong to be easily homogenized by the operations of a parliamentary system of government and plurality electoral system in single-member constituencies.[11] That was why the Constituent Assembly decided to combine parliamentary principle with a moderate dose of federal principle of government. Indeed, India's highly centralized constitutional system itself has come under a cloud in recent decades. To take the political system to a new dynamic equilibrium, we have to contemplate how the new consensus is to be generated. In much of India's history, political consensus existed because of a centrally coercive imperial State allowing a large measure of isolationist autonomy to the civil society, and its sprawling domains of dominant castes and communities. In the Gandhian era, political consensus was mainly the product of a hegemonic mass movement of national liberation from the British Raj. In the Nehru era, it was the product of the party system of Congress pluralism and dominance. In the Indira Gandhi era, it was the product of the centralized Congress, predominance often locked in confrontations with the judiciary and populistic extra-parliamentary mass movements.

One may delineate at least two approaches to a new consensus in the post-Emergency era, leaving aside secessionist solutions or a completely new, second republic. Rajni Kothari (1976, p. 106) has been pointing towards an alternative model which is essentially a plea for renewal of the original model whose central thrust "was *the integration of social and regional diversities into a common framework on the basis of not an imposed mechanical unity but of eliciting a new solidarity in which the various diversities found meaning*" (p.41). In the series of institutional reforms suggested by Kothari, the most basic is creating a more federalized parliament with a stronger second chamber giving equal and effective representation to all States, small and big. A more conservative approach to the problem of federalizing India's predominantly parliamentary system is found in the Report of the Sarkaria Commission on Centre-State Relations. Instead of dividing the parliamentary power more evenly between the popular and the federal chambers, the Commission has recommended a series of advisory independent federal instrumentalities with constitutional status and regular secretariat, e.g. National Economic Development Council, Inter-Governmental Council, Planning Commission and Finance Commission. Besides, the Commission has also recommended some ways of expanding the divisible pool of revenue resources between the Centre and the State. Moreover, it has also *exhorted a reorientation on the part of federal functionaries and normative behaviour respecting State autonomy.*[12]

Implement Before it is Too Late

It is time the Government of India got on with the job of implementing at least the Sarkaria Commission recommendations before it is too late.

There is no point in waiting endlessly for the return of the predominant party system which recedes further into history with the growing industrialization and peripheral politicization of the country. Modernization brings increasing structural differentiation and functional specialization. This is evident, among others, in the *emerging autonomy of major interest/pressure groups from political parties.* The predominant pattern of "colonization" of interest groups by political parties that has been typical of India broadly still continues. But there are new tendencies there now. For example, the 18-month and two-and-a-half-lakh textile workers' strike in Bombay in the early 1980s was spear-headed by a trade union led by Dr. Datta Samant not affiliated with any political party.[13] Moreover, powerful farmers' movements in the 1980s such as those led by Mahendra Singh Tikait in Western U.P. and Sharad Joshi in Maharashtra have also assiduously avoided formal affiliation with any party.[14] *Regional and ethnic identities have, moreover, in recent decades tended to find political articulation through separate parties.* For these reasons, it is more likely for India to make, at some distant date, a rendezvous with a pluralist two-party system than to beat a retreat to the heady Klondike Goldrush of the Nehru era. For though the *federal component of the political system would continue to diversify the party system, the functional imperatives of the parliamentary system would tend to exert a bipolarizing effect on the configuration of parties.*

NOTES

1. The terms ideological and coercive state apparatuses are borrowed from Louis Althusser (1984).
2. The National Front consisting of the Janata Dal, Asom Gana Parishad, Dravida Munnetra Kazhagam, Telugu Desam and Congress-S led by Unnikrishnan jointly campaigned in the parliamentary elections of 1989 and formed a minority government in November that year with the additional parliamentary support of Communist parties and the BJP.
3. The State component of the party system today has become very complex. Classifiable along more than one axis, State politics in India defies any easy typology. At the time of writing (early February 1991), a cursory look reveals a number of States under President's rule (e.g. Punjab, Jammu and Kashmir, Tamil Nadu, Andhra and Karnataka and some North-Eastern States under the Congress, Bihar and Orissa under the Janata Dal, U.P., Haryana and Gujarat under the Janata Dal (Samajwadi), the BJP, some North-Eastern States under some tribal parties and coalition governments, and so on.
4. I have outlined the structural and ideological properties of this new party system

and placed it in a tentative evolutionary context elsewhere (M.P. Singh, 1990 and 1990a).

5. See Subhas Kashyap (1969).
6. This was in the wake of the crisis in the National Front Government stemming from the withdrawal of support from it by the BJP following the Government's determined bid not to let Advani's *Rath Yatra* to proceed to Ayodhya (ironically meaning a non-warring city) to begin construction of the *Ram Mandir* on the site of the Babri Masjid supposedly built in the 16th century on the site of a Ram-janambhumi (birth-place) temple. Historian R. S. Sharma (1990) does not find any solid evidence for the conjecture that a Ram temple was demolished to build the *masjid* at the dispute site.

   The Speaker's ruling recognized the new party, Janata Dal (Samajwadi), formed by JD dissenters led by Chandra Shekhar and Devi Lal as a separate parliamentary party, as it comprised more than one-third of the membership of the original JD. However, he ruled that only 28 of them had clearly conveyed their decision to him on November 5, 1990: the other 8, including 5 ministers, were — disqualified from Lok Sabha membership as there was some ambiguity about their position on November 5. Meanwhile the Delhi High Court stayed the November 5 order to JD leader V.P. Singh expelling 25 party MPs apparently with a mala fide intent of denying the dissenters the protection of at least "one-third' stipulation of the Tenth Schedule of the Constitution to winnow dissenters from defectors. The Court, however, ruled that the power of deciding whether the anti-defection law applied to the JD belonged to the Speaker. The Speaker's and Court's rulings came at the fage-end of the winter session of Parliament. See *The Times of India* (New Delhi, Metro), January 12, 1991.
7. For these models, see Arendt Lijphart (1984).
8. *The Times of India* (New Delhi, Metro), January 26, 1991. p.1.
9. While most parties and leaders have remained cool to the former proposition, the latter is generally discounted by political science and legal fraternities (M.P. Singh, 1981, A.G. Noorani, 1989).
10. I am indebted for this observation to Douglas Verney made in the course of a conversation with me at the India International Centre, New Delhi, in late January, 1991.
11. On theorized consequences of the parliamentary and electoral systems for the nature of the party system, see Leon D. Epstein (1967, Ch. 2) and Douglas Rae (1971).
12. (Sarkaria) Commission Report on Centre-State Relations (1988).
13. See Rajni Bakshi (1986).
14. See Staffan Lindberg (1990).

REFERENCES

Althousser, Louis (1984). *Essays on Ideology*, London & New York: Verso.

Bakshi, Rajni (1986). *The Long Laul: The Bombay Textile Workers Strike*, Bombay: Build Documentation Centre.

Epstein, Leon (1967). *Political Parties in Western Democracies*, New York: Praeger Publishers.

Galanter, Marc (1984). *Competing Equalities: Law and Backward Classes in India,* Delhi: Oxford University Press.

Government of India (1988). *Commission of Centre-State Relations:* (Chairman: Justice R.S. Sarkaria), Parts I & II. Nasik: Government of India Press.

Government of India (1981). *Backward Classes Commission Report* (Chairman B.P. Mandal), 7 volumes in 2. New Delhi: Controller of Publications.

Government of India (1988). *Commission of Centre-State Relations:* (Chairman: Justice R.S. Sarkaria), Parts I & II, Nasik: Government of India Press.

Kashyap, Subhas C. (1969). *Politics of Defection.* Delhi: National Publishing House.

Kothari, Rajni (1970). *Politics in India,* Boston: Little Brown & Co. (Simultaneously published in India by Orient Longman).

Kothari, Rajni (1976). *Democratic Polity and Social Change in India: Crisis and Opportunities.* New Delhi: Allied Publishers.

Lijphart, Arendt (1984). *Democracies: Patterns of Majoritarian and Consensus Government in Twenty-one Countries.* New Haven: Yale University Press.

Lindberg, Staffan (1990). "Civil Society Against the State? Farmers' Agitation and New Social Movements in India"; XII World Congress of Sociology, RC 09, Madrid, 9-13 July 1990.

Noorani, A.G. (1989). The Presidential System: The Indian Debate. New Delhi: Sage Publications.

Rae, Douglas (1971). *Political Consequences of Electoral Laws.* New Haven: Yale University Press.

Sartori, Giovanni (1976). *Parties and Party Systems: A Framework for Analysis,* Vol.1. Cambridge: Cambridge University Press.

Sharma, R. S. (1990). *Communal History and Ram's Ayodhya,* New Delhi: People Publishing House.

Singh, M.P. (1981). "Presidential System for India? a Note on the Recent Rethinking", *Journal of Constitutional and Parliamentary Studies,* Vol. XIV, No. 1 (January-March), pp. 1-6.

11

ETHNICITY AND NATIONAL INTEGRATION – Meaning, Concept and Issues

S.M. DUBEY

The conflict between protagonists of the ethnic identity and autonomy on the one hand and the extension of spheres of the nation-state, accelerated process of nation-building and integration on the other is a global phenomenon.

Class, ethnicity, nation and their relationship have emerged as an important field of inquiry in contemporary social sciences.

In spite of the wide application of concepts of "ethnicity" and "integration", there is a lack of rigour in their use. The growing assertions of black identity in the USA, rivalry between the French and the English-speaking population in Canada, demand of self-determination in Northern Ireland, challenges posed by cultural diversities in nation-building in newly independent countries of Asia and Africa, recent developments in the USSR and Yugoslavia are some of the major factors which have aroused interests of social scientists in the analysis of issues pertaining to ethnicity and national integration.

The literal meaning of "ethnicity" is heathen nation, "heathen superstitions". The ethnic refers to "nations" which are "heathen" or "pagan" and races (*Oxford English Dictionary*). Before the Second World War, it was used to denote marginal non-Christian communities living in Western societies.

Sociologically, ethnicity may be defined as an ascriptive bond (Parsons: 1961) and a descent group (Jackson: 1984). Max Weber almost equated "ethnic consciousness" with tribalism which is characterized by a low degree of rationality. There is similarity as well as difference between ethnicity, kinship and group. Kinship includes blood ties also, whereas, ethnic identity is determined by birth. Ethnic groups work as interest groups also. The modern social system is extremely complex and similarly its process of integration is also very complex. The term "integration" implies the existence of multiple entities and the process of their coming together and becoming a part of the whole. Integration is viewed as a property of systems in which different connected components interact with each other and form a relationship (Henry Teune in Gisvani Sartori, *Social Science Concepts,* Sage, 1984, pp. 235-64). There are social, cultural, economic and political aspects of integration in a system (society, State, federal polity and modern market). In the context of national integration, though social and cultural components are also very significant yet the major emphasis is on the political dimension of integration.

Ethnic groups arise and persist by virtue of boundary creation and maintenance (Barth: 1969). The bases of ethnicity are race, colour, language, customs, religion, caste, tribe and region. History, geography, economy, power and culture are major variables which explain group differences, separateness and boundaries.

In this context, it is noteworthy that the processes of the boundary maintenance and the expansion of boundaries operate simultaneously in a system. Societal integration and State formation are closely linked with the expansion of boundaries. In this process, the small groups, entities and collectivities become the part of a larger entity. This is a process as well as a State.

Integration promotes a sense of belongingness among smaller entities with the larger system. Historically, this process has been achieved by *persuasive* as well as *coercive* methods. In most of the cases, a blending of both methods is visible.

Ethnic mobilization is closely linked with ethnic consciousness, goals, means, organization and symbols. The ethnic consciousness may be dormant or awakened (Jackson: 1984). Ethnic mobilization takes place whenever there is a fear or threat (real or imaginary) to the cultural identity, a sense of economic deprivation and a strong sentiment against political domination by others.

The contemporary process of ethnic mobilization in closely linked with the formation of nation-states – consisting of diverse socio-political groups and different regions. This heterogeneity of components in a system (whole) makes people conscious of the majority–minority relationship, dialectics of deprivation–domination and the resentment towards an uneven nature of development and regional imbalances. These factors quite often lead to ethnic movements.

The typologies of the ethnic movements can be explained in the larger frame of identity-integration, and system-sub-system relationship. There are two distinct points of views in this regard. The first group which believes in integration thinks that there is a system (whole) and it has its components (parts, smaller entities). The major emphasis of this group is always on unity, harmony, cohesion, solidarity, integration accommodation and assimilation. This group, starting from accommodation ("liberal" notion of integration) to assimilation (extreme form of integration), stresses on different degrees of integration.

The emphasis of the second group (minority, smaller entities) is sometimes on parallel, equidistant identities, and separateness. The issues of their discontent may be cultural, economic or political. Depending on the intensity of their demands, their movements may be for cultural safeguards, limited autonomy for controlling their social, economic, and political affairs, self-determination and secession. These questions are linked with the goals of the ethnic movements, which may create four logical typologies of cultural safeguards, autonomy, self-determination and secession.

From the point of view of means, the typologies of ethnic movements may be divided into social protests, constitutional fight, violent struggle and insurgency. From the point of view of the dominant groups, the ethnic movements are generally termed as separatist or secessionist.

The relationship between the rise of different ethnic groups and the national sentiments are also visible in history in the shape of early dynastic State formations, rise of nationalism in the 18th, 19th centuries, and adoption of the principle of self-determination after the First World War and increasing conflict between ethnicity and nationalism.

The major components of modernization such as education, urbanization, industrialization, technological advancement, physical, occupations, social mobility and mass-media are supposed to reduce the intensity of ethnic identities and separateness. They have not fully succeeded in reducing separateness.

12

ETHNICITY AND NATIONAL INTEGRATION — A Gandhian Perspective

VIJAY RANJAN DUTTA

The diversities of the Indian subcontinent and the search for identity by different ethnic groups in democratic political processes pose a challenge to the centralized structure of the Indian polity. In order to meet this challenge the Indian political system tried to solve the problem of ethnicity centering round the linguistic identity. Accordingly it was on the basis of the recommendations of the State Reorganization Commission submitted to the Union Government in 1956 that fourteen States were demarcated and carved out to meet the linguistic demands of different regions. This was an attempt to foster the cultural identity of ethnic groups living in new States within the broad framework of the process of democratic nation-building. Another attempt to preserve the cultural identity of ethnic groups was evident in the North-East region when Nagaland, Meghalaya, Manipur, Arunachal Pradesh, Tripura and Mizoram got statehood in phases. A new Punjab State was also carved out in 1966 on a linguistic basis to meet the demand of Punjabi Suba raised by the Akali leaders and thereby the Sikhs constituted a majority of 62.2 per cent of the population while the Hindus formed 37.54 per cent.

Recently, the Darjeeling Hill Council was constituted in West Bengal as per the Act passed by the State Legislature to promote the cultural identity of the Nepali ethnic group. The grievances of some tribes and their demand for Bodoland in Assam is also under consideration of the Union Government and the Assam Government. The Union Home Ministry is also looking into the problems of the tribal people in Bihar and their demand for a separate Jharkhand State within the Indian Union.

The political process for meeting the ethnic problem appears to be encouraging. Nevertheless, the ethnicity problem is not over and it has taken new shapes and turbulent turns in Assam, Punjab and Jammu and Kashmir. The militancy of the movements with active involvement of the youths in these States at the periphery of India either in the shape of ethnic identity or in the form of greater State autonomy has posed a crisis situation in the nation. It appears that the ethnicity problem veers round cultural-cum-regional assertion and its rightful place in the nation.

Thus, the ethnicity problem persists and the present structure of the polity has not been able to solve it. It seems that there are four basic reasons for the failure: (i) Hierarchy-based colonial administration borrowed from the West and thereby creating patron-client relation in society; (ii) Gap between elite and mass–a by-product of centralized decision-making process; (iii) Equation of power in polity not balanced leading to deprivation on the part of some ethnic groups: (iv) Youth power not utilized properly for the cause of the nation and thereby youths are attracted to militant ethnic movements for their welfare and betterment.

The identity problem of some ethnic groups is also precipitated by economic and political threats posed by migrants. For example, the people of Assamese origin apprehend that their relative number will decrease in their own State. They feel that their identity is likely to be overshadowed by the migrants very soon. They may be deprived of political power even in their own State. It is also noteworthy that only 10 per cent people of Assamese origin are engaged in the Central services in Assam like railway, banks, postal services, etc. Such identity crisis creates the problem of sub-nationalism combined with violence and terrorist forces.

The fear of the tribal population of being outnumbered by the non-tribals persists in the Chota Nagpur region of Bihar also. Consciousness of tribal identity and the desire for a greater share in power appears to be the motivating force in tribal politics. They demand a separate Jharkhand State within the Indian Union consisting of 27 tribes spread over 16 districts in four States–Bihar, West Bengal, Orissa and Madhya Pradesh. It shows assertion of ethnic-cum-regional identity for sharing political power in a separate Jharkhand State.

The new State of Punjab was carved out on a linguistic basis in 1966. But the politics of the State took a new turn in 1973 by the Akali demand of greater autonomy to the State where the "Centre's interference would be restricted to Defence, Foreign Relation, Currency and General communication." Besides, the party also demanded certain religious concessions. The Akali Dal leadership argued that Sikh identity cannot be maintained without combining religion with politics. Obviously, the Sikh identity aspires for greater sharing of power in the polity.

The process of national integration depends neither on a strong centralized polity nor on the development model of the West. We have to search indigenous symbols of integration. For this, the nation has to derive vigour from the value-concept of non-violence. Unless individual virtue of non-violence transforms into social virtue, the dynamics of strengthening a cohesive nation appears to be disturbed. To Gandhi, "...non-violence is not merely a personal virtue. It is also a social virtue to be cultivated like the other virtues".[1]

It is the paradigm of non-violence which keeps the nation together, and the spirit of participatory democracy alive. At first glance, the approach appears to be utopian but the crisis-situation makes it imperative to weave out certain operational parts of the paradigm. There are four components of the paradigm of non-violence to promote national integration: (i) Leadership role; (ii) Restructuring of polity; (iii) Dynamics of non-violence and series of dialogue in the decision-making process; and (iv) Relation between culture and politics.

(i) **Role of Leadership**

Man often fails to transcend the frontiers of caste, religion, dialect and region for the larger interest of a cohesive nation. In this context, the role of leadership is significant in transforming the narrow range of individual psyche into taking a broader vision of collective ethics and communitarian society.

At present, elites of political parties lack skill to evolve indigenous categories of national symbols which can create harmony between national identity and different ethnic identities. It was the quality of Mahatma Gandhi's leadership which tried to project indigenous symbols of non-violence like *Khadi, Swadeshi*, etc. which had a wider appeal to masses in different parts of the country. These symbols aroused the masses for involvement in the task of national independence. The style of Gandhi's leadership also made attempts to bridge the communication gap between elite and mass. It was noteworthy that he fought for the cause of the downtrodden irrespective of ethnic or regional bias. Gandhi had the capacity to make the genuine cause of a particular section an all-India issue and thereby drew the sympathy of people of the whole country. His view on crucial questions was never branded as parochial. His method of mass contact by undertaking intensive tours of different parts of the country was full of potentiality to bridge the communication gap between elite and mass. Today, leaders depend more on mass media rather than on mass contact for a personal relationship with the common man. No doubt, when the crisis is deep, a drive for mass contact is launched by some political parties. Since the programme is taken up at a very late stage, its impact on the people is not effective and widespread. In fact, political parties have reduced themselves to a mere electoral machine. No serious attempt has been made by most of the parties to institutionalize different forms of elite mass relationships. The crisis-situation demands that one communicates with the people like Gandhi for inculcating sentiments of fellow-feeling and brotherhood. The leadership will have to provide goals and ideals for redirecting human energy and resources to a more constructive and national end and purpose. It would also be worthwhile to weave a pattern of "constructive non-violence" into basic activities of human lives. It is essential to put into practice the nineteen-fold constructive work programme as devised by Gandhi for socio-economic transformation. Such a programme can provide the basis for non-violent social relationships. New items can be added according to exigencies of the present crisis. The successful application of a constructive work programme[2] like eradication of untouchability, uplift of the Scheduled Tribes, voluntary prohibition, communal harmony, etc., requires training of dedicated workers and experiments of non-violence with continuity.

(ii) **Restructuring of Polity**

It is a matter of debate whether the centralized parliamentary system of Indian polity can tackle the diverse problems of the vast nation. Politics today is confined to Central and State levels of governance. Political parties rely on the charisma of a few top leaders. This creates a wide gulf between State and Society. As a result, the initiative of society for building the nation is lost. Reviewing the working of the Indian polity Jayaprakash Narayan stated: "The truth must be faced that the people have not been able to experience the sensation of Swaraj. It is only the very thin layer of the educated middle class, and even of them only those directly engaged in political activity, who are involved in the working of our democracy."[3] This implies that majority of the people don't have any stake in political power. And certain ethnic-cum-regional groups still remain at the periphery and are far away from the centre of political power.

Although emphasis has been laid by some social scientists on "district" as the third tier of federal polity, the pyramidal structuring of power is still the core of Indian polity. There is hierarchy of power with higher and lower levels of structure. We must accept the fact that hierarchy and integration cannot go together and thus it seems very difficult to promote a cohesive spirit for building a strong nation. Mahatma Gandhi conceived autonomous units at different levels which would be organically linked together by a principle of integration which he calls "an oceanic circle". It is relevant to cite Gandhi's views on the "oceanic circle":

> "In this structure composed of innumerable villages there will be everwidening, never ascending circles. Life will not be a pyramid with the apex sustained by the bottom. But it will be an oceanic circle whose centre will be the individual always ready to perish for the village, the latter ready to perish for the circle of villages, till at last, the whole becomes one life composed of individuals, never aggressive in their arrogance but ever humble sharing the majesty of the oceanic circle of which they are integral units. Therefore, the outermost circumference will not wield power to crush the inner circle but give strength to all within and derive its own from the centre."[4]

The framework of oceanic circle ensures a measure of autonomy and self-reliance at different levels for involving the people. In a way, this is an attempt to establishment what G.D.H. calls "little democracies" at different levels and thereby the present form of centralized parliamentary democracy is replaced by multiple centres of power and decision-making. Since the conceptual framework of the oceanic circle ensures dignity, equal status and autonomy to individuals, ethnic groups and regions, the problem of alienation will not arise and thereby different ethnic groups and units of the nation will work in unison for restructuring the polity and should be considered as one of the basic conditions for national integration. This may require drastic changes in the Indian Constitution and this is a matter of debate.

(iii) **Dynamics of Non-violence and Series of Dialogue**

There is a qualitative difference between violent and non-violent means adopted for the achievement of one's identity. Eric Erikson holds the view that violence can achieve only "negative identity". This identity is based on distrust, hate and exclusion of the person or group that is target of violence. The Gandhian technique of non-violence is humane which fosters an "all-inclusive identity". The perspective of this identity is based on trust, love and harmonious relationships among the actors of non-violence.

The experiment of non-violence in social relationships is based on the principle of stimulus and response which acts upon man's activities. Richard B. Gregg has examined the efficacy of non-violence in this context. He contends that the process of stimulus and response can enhance man's emotional and moral faculties. Since potentiality for good exists in every living person, growth in response to gentle, appropriate and repeated stimuli is more enduring than any form of political government, economic action and force. The process may not yield quick result because it requires a series of repeated experiments.[5] Further, the prevailing concept of human relationship involves dominance of one person and subordination of the other at various levels. The system prevails in all spheres of life. This has resulted in different types of conflicts. The principle of non-violence and submission offers an alternative system of relationships based on "integration".[6] In this pattern, each person or unit is in search of a common goal in activities which are mutually satisfying to all concerned. Each one shows trust and expects trust from others. Such interaction is in no way a compromise but progress and adaptation for the achievement of common goal.

The theoretical perspective on the dynamics of non-violence can be applied meaningfully in the context of demands of ethnic movements raised in some States of India. The role of leadership is significant to operationalize the virtues of non-violence in our social processes. Leaders of political parties will have to keep themselves above the electoral gains and loss and they will have to adopt a holistic approach to view the crucial problems which, at times, hinder the cohesiveness of the nation.

Dialogue is the *sine qua non* of non-violent approach to the nation-building process in a large subcontinent like India. For this, some institutions like Zonal Councils and National Integration Council have been created. They functioned in their early phase but later on they were allowed to become moribund. However, these institutions were revived during the eighties. Further, the Indian Constitution envisages the provision of setting up of an Inter-State Council in Article 263. It was after a long debate in political circles that the Inter-State Council was set up by the National Front Government at the Centre in 1990. But the relevant question is that meetings of such institutions are not held at regular intervals and their venues are often kept at Delhi or in some State capital. It appears that the meetings of such institutions are mere rituals without any impact on the nation-building process. In this context, the State has to establish linkages with voluntary organizations working in different areas of the country. In fact, political parties fail to reach the poor, the landless, the Dalit, the Adivasis and others except at the time of elections. Therefore, the role of voluntary organizations is important in a country like India which has diversities with a number of socio-economic problems.

(iv) Culture and Politics

It is noteworthy that the dynamics of non-violence for resolving crucial problems facing a nation requires certain basic human values. Fortunately, the Indian Constitution provides a precise and valuable Preamble as its introductory section which enunciates human values like justice, equality, liberty and fraternity. Later, principles like socialism, secularism and integrity have been added to the Preamble by an act of amendment to the Constitution in 1976. The addition of the word "integrity" to the Preamble was considered to be significant and, therefore, the Constitution (Forty second Amendment) Act, 1976, introduced Article 5A in Part IV-A to the text of the Constitution entitled "Fundamental Duties" and one of the duties is to "uphold and protect sovereignty, unity and integrity of India". Further, the Preamble of the Constitution aptly refers to the operational dynamics of the word "fraternity": "Fraternity assuring the dignity of the individual and the (unity and integrity of the nation)". It signifies that the Indian Constitution aspires to maintain a balance between the dignity of the individual and the unity and integrity of the nation. Obviously, the value-concept of "fraternity" specifically mentioned in the Preamble of the Constitution can subserve the cohesive spirit of the nation. The application of the value-concept in terms of policy measures cannot be the responsibility of political leaders alone. In fact, the value-concept like "fraternity" touches the culture of the people living in different parts of our country. Promoting "fraternity" in the framework of culture is a delicate task and this can be fulfilled by social reformers, intellectuals and artists who have a wider vision. The decision of the Government of

India to set up seven cultural centres in different zones of the country seems to be in the right direction to promote the culture of each and every area. In a way, this leads to demetropolization of culture and thereby artists in particular and people in general living in different parts of the country will be able to appreciate the cultural dynamics of human existence. The nation also needs poets like Tagore, Subramanya Bharati, Maithili Sharan Gupta and Dinkar who tried to promote cultural unity of the nation by their poetic genius. Further, the *Bhakti* movement led by Kabir, Mirabai and others also provided a fertile base for the creation of a humanist culture which can form the core of India's "national unity". India requires "a cultural mosaic" perspective[7] and policy measures in order to nurture a national culture by stimulating constant interaction among the artists of different regions.

Today, India needs a policy on culture with the people's participation at different levels of the polity for socio-economic transformation of the entire nation. For national integration a renaissance is essential and it would be relevant if the people at the periphery of the country come forward for evolving indigenous symbols which will promote cultural unity. The heroes, folklore, art and culture of certain peripheral groups and regions should be recorded in major languages and attempts be made to identify new symbols for nation-building purposes. For example, Birsa Munda, who fought against the British rulers in the Ranchi area and died as a martyr, should be considered as a national hero. Similar is the case of Subramanya Bharati, the renowned Tamil poet, who composed most of his poems on Indian nationalism. The contributions of such eminent persons should form party of a new renaissance for the cultural unity of the country.

NOTES

1. M.K. Gandhi. *Village Swaraj* (compiled by H.N. Vyas), Navajivan Publishing House, Ahmedabad, 1963, p. 53.
2. For details see, M.K. Gandhi, *Constructive Programme—Its meaning and place*, Navajivan, Ahmedabad, 1961 (reprinted).
3. Jayaprakash Narayan. *Swaraj for the People*, A.B. Sarva Seva Sangh, Varanasi, 1961, p.2.
4. M.K. Gandhi. *Village Swaraj*, op.cit., p. 70.
5. For details see, Richard B. Garg, *The Power of Non-Violence*, Navajivan, Ahmedabad, 1949, (New Edition), pp.105-9.
6. *Ibid.*, pp. 125-26.
7. P.C. Joshi. "Role of Culture in Social Transformation and National Integration", *Economic and Political Weekly*, Vol. XXI, No. 28, July 12, 1986, p. 1231.

13

PARTICIPATION : Key to Integration

M. ARAM

The subject of the Seminar, "Ethnic Identity and National Integration", is of great public importance and serious academic interest. Today we witness divisive tendencies and fissiparous forces operating in our country. We face serious challenges to national unity and integration.

The proposition I would like to support is: "No integration without participation". Prof. Sachchidananda stated this in the course of his presentation. I shall speak from my experience of the Nagaland Peace Mission of which Shri Jayaprakash Narayan was a distinguished architect. I shall explain how participation is necessary for integration.

Nagaland is an excellent case of "Ethnic Identity and National Integration". True, the Naga people have a special identity and their concern was to preserve it. In the beginning they were only disparate tribes without a unifying factor. But the *outsiders started perceiving the Nagas as* one entity. Later when the *British established their administration,* the Naga identity developed further. As *Christianity* spread among the various tribes, that was another uniting factor. Thus the Naga identity became a powerful reality. On the other hand, Naga links with India were rather weak, almost non-existent.

"Common Culture" and "Freedom Movement" were the two powerful factors that unified India. The Indian identity rested very much on these two factors. Unfortunately both these were lacking in the case of Nagaland. Further the British followed a policy of keeping Nagaland in isolation apart from the country.

Identity Crisis

In such a situation World War II descended upon the Naga Hills in the year 1945. It caused an acute identity crisis. When Indian independence came in 1947, it further aggravated the identity crisis. When Mr.

A.Z. Phizo, Naga Nationalist leader, met Mahatma Gandhi, he said he wanted to declare Nagaland independent on August 14, 1947. Gandhiji asked, "Why wait till August 14? I declared myself independent long ago". Mr Phizo said they were apprehensive that Indian Army would take over and start shooting the Nagas. Gandhiji became serious and declared: "No, that cannot be. I will come to Kohima and they should shoot me first before they shoot any Naga." This statement of Gandhiji made a powerful impact upon the Naga Delegation.

Nevertheless, when the first general elections were held in Nagaland, there was a total boycott. No Naga voted. This non-participation in the political process was a fact which no one could ignore. Shri B.P. Chaliha, President of the Assam Pradesh Congress Committee, toured the Naga Hills and told the people: "I respect your sentiment of independence. But I advise you to be in the Union of India". The sincerity of Chaliha impressed the Nagas. The problem continued, however. In 1956 violence broke out. Violence and counter-violence caused immense suffering to the common people.

Constitutional Safeguards

Pandit Jawaharlal Nehru responded constructively and agreed to form a separate Nagaland State in 1961 with special constitutional safeguards mentioned in Article 371A. Still, violence did not cease. It was not a triangular situation in which the Underground, the State Government and the Central Government were the three parties. To put an end to the violence and suffering, the Nagaland Church Council formed a Peace Mission in 1964. The first success of the Peace Mission was to bring about a cessation of hostilities of "ceasefire". The ceasefire was very popular. As a Naga leader graphically put it, "The ceasefire line runs through the heart of every Naga."

Shri Jayaprakash Narayan played an outstanding role in the talks between the Underground and the Government. Unfortunately the talks did not yield positive results since both sides reiterated their well-known positions. The Peace Mission came forward to do the delicate job of suggesting a formula for a political settlement. This, too, did not help.

It was a period of "peace without settlement". The situation became more and more normal because of the continuous extension of the ceasefire. *The factors which were in favour of the ceasefire and peace were many and strong. But the factors in favour of political settlement were few and weak. Thus the public opinion had to be nourished in support of peace and settlement.*

Mass Participation

Fortunately the political process continued to operate in Nagaland. There were periodic elections and they were free and fair. There was "mass participation in the democratic process", to use the phrase of Prof. Anirudha Gupta. This Naga people saw for themselves that they could make and unmake governments. Indeed the erstwhile opposition party, which was supposed to be "pro-underground", formed the government.

The efforts for settlement were intensified and they were crowned with success in the form of the Shillong Peace Accord in 1975. The underground accepted the Union of India "of their own volition". They also deposited their arms "at appointed places" and "the other issues" were kept open for future talks and settlement.

Along with the political process, development process too continued to operate with increasing mass participation. Both contributed to the normalization of the situation in Nagaland. Greater participation by the people in politics and development resulted in the Naga getting closer to the rest of the country and getting integrated with the larger whole, without losing their cultural identity.

A prominent leader from Delhi suggested to a Naga leader "to join the national mainstream". He replied: "Sir, we are already in the national mainstream–only we find ourselves in troubled waters.

National Scene

May I now turn to the national scene. The present situation is that the Political Process in the country has reached a state of acute crisis. Thirdly, I may add, the Education Process too has reached a state of acute crisis.

Thus there is a crisis situation in the country. What is the way out? The proposition I would like to advance is: "Change the system. Make it more participatory."

We need changes in the political system to make our democracy more participatory. We need changes in the economic system to make development *more* participatory. We need radical changes in the education system to make learning *more* participatory.

May I first take up the political system.

Political System

The party system is losing its credibility. In India the two-party system has not taken root. We have a multi-party system. What happened in the last two years is something unprecedented. There was "a minority party with majority support". It lasted for about a year. Then there was another minority party, still smaller group, which formed the government with the support of a majority party. This government lasted only a few months.

The post-election scenario was uncertain. If no party gets a clear majority, then what? Coalition government is possible but a weak coalition cannot produce a stable government.

In these circumstances, we need participatory politics. We need a third tier of government which is *Panchayati Raj*. Unfortunately the Constitution amendment to establish Panchayati Raj could not be passed for lack of just three votes in the Rajya Sabha. But even now it is not too late. No party is against the Panchayati Raj. If through consensus Panchayati Raj could be established, then there will be popular participation in the political process at the grass-root level.

On the other hand, at the national level, we should think of a "national government". The philosophy of India is "Unity in Diversity". Different viewpoints are accommodated and a consensus is developed. The consensus is the basis for action. The Indian political system should be restructured to make for participatory democracy, i.e. Panchayati Raj at the grassroot level and National Government at the national level.

Mahatma Gandhi envisioned a decentralized political system and he called it an "Oceanic Circle". Here is his famous passage:

> "In this structure composed of innumerable villages there will be ever-widening, never ascending circles. Life will not be a pyramid with the apex sustained by the bottom. But it will be an oceanic circle whose centre will be the individual always ready to perish for the village, the latter ready to perish for the circle of villages, till at last, the whole becomes one life composed of individuals, *never aggressive in their arrogance but ever humble sharing the majesty of the oceanic circle of which they are integral units.* Therefore, the outermost circumference will not wield power to crush the inner

circle but give strength to all within and derive its own from the centre."

Shri Jayaprakash Narayan quotes this famous passage and says: "Gandhi's ideas of decentralization are usually brushed aside as being irrelevant or not depends very much on what one wants, what values one holds dear."

Development Process

The crisis situation in the field of development is that even now about forty per cent of our people are below the poverty line. Population growth continues inexorably. Over two per cent growth rate is rather serious. Every year 16 million are added.

Unemployment increases rather than decreases. We can achieve cent per cent employment or full employment. We have many successful micro experiments to our credit. There are villages, even areas, where, through *participatory* planning and development, cent per cent employment, zero per cent poverty and zero per cent population growth have been achieved.

But these are only *micro successes.* What we need is a macro *breakthrough.* To achieve this, the development process should be reconceptualized and restructured.

We need statutory planning bodies at the district level, block level and village level. There should be District Planning Commissions and Block and Village Planning Committees. They should be statutory with sufficient authority to plan for area development.

The Panchayati Raj bodies should have adequate resources at their disposal. Participatory Democracy and Participatory Development go hand in hand.

Education Process

In education too, we need radical changes. There has been tremendous quantitative expansion. In 1950 we had only 20 universities. Today we have 170 universities with about 7,000 colleges. But the situation is not satisfactory. There has been a sharp decline in quality and standards.

Besides, social reluctance is not there. Education contributes to the problem rather than to the solution. The large number of unemployed graduates are a sad commentary on the university system. What is worse, they are *unemployable graduates.* By churning out lakhs of unemployable young men with degrees, the university system is doing a grievous disservice to society.

When I was the Vice-Chancellor of Gandhigram Rural University, we held up a motto before the young students: *"Be Part of the Solution not of the Problem."*

We had a national debate on the basis of a status paper, "The Challenge of Education". We developed a New Education Policy through a participatory process. But the problem has always been of implementation. To tackle this problem, we developed a Programme of Action, but the Programme of Action cannot be implemented unless we have committed teachers and adequate resources. Unfortunately both are lacking. The implementation process has been halting and slow.

So we need radical approaches in the field of education. Learning, to be creative, should be participatory. It should be student-centred. In the same way, teaching, to be creative should be participatory too. The teacher should be the designer, executor and evaluator of the curriculum.

Global Scene

May I turn to the global scene. The subject of identity and integration should also be considered in the international context. Dr. Ali Ashraf referred to SAARC as a possible framework within which the nations of South Asia can maintain their identities and still cooperate for regional development. Taking the cue from the European Community, South Asia should develop into a powerful regional framework.

Tremendous changes are taking place on the world scene. Momentous developments are sweeping the Soviet Union. Glasnost and perestroika mean more openness and more participation. A new global order, the right one, should emerge. India has a significant role to play. India, in the year, has been playing a leading role in the development of the global community. India should play a leading role in the future too. India's special contribution will be to help create a "non-violent, nuclear weapon-free world".

The world expects a great deal from India. Arnold Toynbee said that the *modern period which had a "Western* beginning" should have an "Indian ending". Toynbee says:

"It is already becoming clear that a chapter which had a Western

> beginning will have an Indian ending if it is not to end in the self-destruction of the human race.....
>
> "At this supremely dangerous moment in human history, the only way of salvation for mankind is the Indian way –Emperor Asoka's and Mahatma's testimony to the harmony of religions.
>
> "Here we have an attitude and spirit that can make it possible for the human race to grow together into a single family–and, in the Atomic Age, this is the only alternative to destroying ourselves."

As we move towards the end of this century and the dawn of the 21th century, a clear vision of the destiny of India and a clear vision of the Future World Order are necessary. And we must work, with renewed inspiration, for national unity and integration in the larger context of global peace and international understanding.

14

RAMJANAMBHOOMI-BABARI MASJID CONTROVERSY:
A Non-Governmental Solution

RAMJEE SINGH

There is no other issue demanding our attention as much as the "Ramjanambhoomi-Babari Masjid Conflict" in the context of National Unity and Integration, because it has got linked with the large sections of one of the minorities of India, namely, Muslims. Apart from that the political overtones that it has acquired have rendered its untanglement even more difficult. The picture of the latest elections is there to see how the two warring parties made and unmade political fortunes. Under such circumstances, to hope for a solution from the political leadership or the administration is to ask for the moon. The politics of vote banks is going to tangle it even further. The kind of situation in which the political leadership and administration finds itself, it is virtually impossible to expect a clear-cut and strong polity out of them. Of course for the sake of mere rituals we may keep on and on with some directionless and endless "dialogues", or even clandestine parleys. This small question has been fed with so much of fuel of communalism and politicization that our attention does not turn towards the real issues of starvation, unemployment and price rise. Along with the masses the political parties have also so much polarized that a consensus can hardly emerge among them.

I am impelled by these reasons to think along with you regarding a non-administrative solution. This does not mean that I have a "touch-me-not" attitude towards politics, and consider a non-governmental solution sacrosanct. On the contrary I understand the discouraging limitations of non-governmental solutions. Nevertheless, it seems to me that a non-governmental solution/alternative does not have the political (ideological) commitment or polarization which is there in the political leadership.

I had requested Acharya Tulsi to arbitrate in this matter and arranged for talks between him and Rajmata Scindia and Sayed Shahabuddin three years ago. I had also tried to attract the attention of the intellectuals in a seminar organized under the auspices of the Nehru Museum through a paper on this subject. But while formally praising the paper, the scholars did not make it a subject of serious discussion. It seems that we intellectuals have shut ourselves into an ivory tower and are completely cut off from the problem facing us.

At that time Sayed Shahabuddin had put forth four alternatives for the solution of the Ramjanambhoomi-Babari Masjid tangle:

1. The Mandir-Masjid issue be untangled by the local people and the leaders.
2. The verdict of the court on this question be accepted.
3. The question be discussed and decided by Parliament.
4. The arbitration of some saint and spiritual personalities of the nation be accepted.

The first suggestion might have proved to be very useful in the earlier stages, but now that the feelings of the people and political leaders all over the nation are so much stirred that this suggestion has some understandable limitations now. Of course on the local level, i.e. in Ayodhya some kind of Shanti Sena or Sadbhavana Samiti may be formed, which may create a soothing effect even outside.

Regarding the second alternative, the BJP-VHP combine has already stated its refusal to accept the verdict, saying that it is a question of faith and, therefore, not subject to the verdict of the court. While this in itself is a powerful argument, but more powerful than this is their assertion that if the administration can bow down to the Muslim communalism by disregarding the Supreme Court verdict on Shahbanu issue, then why double standards are being adopted on this question! Besides, this question has been suspended/delayed in the courts for years. It is a blight on the efficiency of the Indian judiciary that this issue is dumped in the cold storage for such a long period. Due to all these reasons the solution through the court also looks difficult. Although it is expected from the Government that it either requests the Session Court to give its impartial verdict within a month's time or come out with necessary suggestion in this regard.

The third alternative is through Parliamentary debates. Since political parties are sharply polarized on this question, therefore, even if Parliament decides this question on majority basis the issue shall remain unsolved. Of course if Parliament makes a decision on the basis of common consent or consensus, the solution is possible. The present situation necessitates emergence of a consensus, and efforts should be made in this direction. But these efforts shall be capped with success only if some behind-the-curtain parleys are done. I feel that it will be a better idea to speak to leaders like Advaniji and Atalji on this issue in place of simply buldozing the BJP entirely.

The last alternative that is left is arbitration through such agencies or groups as are acceptable to both parties. This has two aspects. Firstly, both the parties have to be persuaded for arbitration. Appeals from compassionate and impartial personalities only can persuade both the parties. This is not easy. Secondly both the parties must have faith in the people making efforts in this direction. For this, such names should be suggested for arbitration whose impartiality, political integrity and patriotism are beyond question. Firstly, both the parties agree for arbitration and in the second stage, consensus emerges regarding the names of the arbitrators. There could be two alternative ways of agreement on the arbitrators:

1. Both the parties agree on a name.
2. Both the parties put forward one or two names each and these in turn choose one more person commonly.

Ideally, a Hindu should propose the name of a Muslim and a Muslim that of a Hindu, or a Hindu propose the name of any Non-Hindu and a Muslim that of any non-Muslim.

Still Not Too Late

In my opinion even at the present time of communal upsurge there are such personalities in the public life of India who shall be readily accepted as arbiters by both the parties. Presently I am giving a list of a few names, of course the list has room for modification: Bharat Ratna Morarji Desai, Bharat Ratna Mother Teresa, Swami Ranganathananda of the Ramakrishna Mission, Dr. Mulkraj Anand, Shri Arif Muhammed Khan, Shri C. Subrahmanium, Mohammad Koya, Shri Gopinath Nayar of the Sarva Seva Sangh, Mrs. Nirmala Gandhi, the only living dauthter-in-law of Mahatma Gandhi, or his great-grandson, Shri Rajmohan Gandhi, Acharya Tulsi, Shankaracharya of Kanchipuram, the Cardinal of Bombay, Dalai Lama, etc.

The task is difficult but not impossible. Especially when other kinds of solutions are more difficult this alternative has to be tried. Granted that all efforts in this direction may prove to be futile, but at least history shall not put the blame on us that those who believed in communal harmony did not do anything concrete. Every well-intended effort paves the way for effective solutions of problems. Besides, only a thorough-going effort can be the key to success.

A small work force may be created at the end of this seminar by the Gandhian Institute of Studies to remove the present stalemate. And the suggestions of the honourable members should be collected and widely circulated through mass-media and other means.

While implementing this immediate planning we should not be oblivions of the permanent solution of the communal problem. For that, programmes at three levels could be adopted.

1. *Inclusion of National Integration, Gandhian Thought, and Peace Education in the Curriculum of Educational Institutions.*

The generation which had seen Gandhi or had taken part in the freedom struggle, communal harmony as one of its cherished values and practised it in day-to-day life is almost gone. The younger generation has no ideal figure to follow. Gandhians after Vinoba and J.P. have become ineffective as a national force. The secularism, of the Left is less of a value and inward loyalty, and is more political. No wonder they form government sometimes with the Muslim League and sometimes with the BJP. Even in cases like Shahbano, it does not remain secular. On the other hand the vacuous minds of the teenagers and youth are increasingly getting influenced by communal bigotry. The best way out is to include subjects relating to communal harmony on every level from the beginning till the end of the educational curriculum. A National Integration Committee should be organized in each educational institution and programmes presented under its auspices. History should be narrated/told in right perspective. To contain the growing violence education and training for non-violence is immediately needed.

2. *Organization of Shanti Sena*

To consider police and para-military forces the only solution to violence, caste or communal, is dangerous for democracy. We have seen enough of the lack of authority and capacity of these police and para-military forces. If democracy has to be saved, if people's initiative has to be salvaged from the volley of bullets, organization of a Shanti Sena comes forward as a permanent and effective solution. It will be practical to have Tarun Shanti Sena and village Shanti Sena on the level of youth and villages. We have communal organizations proliferating among the youths but we have forgotten about the importance of the "Shanti Sena" which was conceptualized by Bapu, Vinoba, J.P . and like.

3. *Dialogue Culture and Acharyakul (Think Tank)*

The possibilities of having dialogues are almost invisible in the nation today. From the streets to Parliament we come across rampant anarchy and a complete breakdown of dialogue. The stage of national consensus has gradually shrunken. The credibility of the Sarvodaya Samaj has been eroded. Vinoba wanted to organize the eminent teachers considering that they would be impartial, fearless and non-malicious. And they would be able to direct the nation on any national problem. This would not only create an all-party national forum but also lesson the party and communal tension. But it is a national misfortune that the intellectuals betray a cruel passivity and inertness. The educated class is the greatest national resource, provided it gets organized. Today the nation must be having thirtysix lakhs teachers, one lakh journalists and literateurs, one lakh jurists and scientists. If they are organized into an *Acharyakul* (Think Tank), they can at least provide a healthy direction to the nation by at least voicing their impartial opinion jointly and publicly. Today instead we are caught in the quagmire of party politics or in the confines of caste and community. I cannot see anyone who will talk of humanity.

Conclusion

Fortunately, in spite of all this tension and venom, no responsible Hindu leader is talking of demolishing the mosque nor is any Muslim talking of not having the temple. Even after being in majority it has dawned upon the Hindus that the socio-political international repercussions of demolishing the mosque would be unfavourable. Similarly the Muslims too have understood the faith of the Hindu community in Ram. The path of confrontation is good for none. We cannot create history by digging the past. Similarly, unjustified appeasing of minorities for the sake of vote banks aid and abets separatist tendencies. Therefore, we must rise above party politics to look for solutions and this is possible. The Hindus and the Muslims either decide to live in peace or make India a perpetual Lebanon. Some who talk of doing away with 12 crore Muslims or punish them should find a legitimate place in a madhouse, but not in a civil society. In the same way the Muslim community will have to proceed speedily towards the mainstream, once the charge of separatism and secessionism has been leveled against it. The Indonesian Muslims do not turn into Hindus if they appreciate the Ramayana and Ramlila, Bangladeshi Muslims do not become *Kafirs* if they study Bengali literature, the Turkish Mohammedans do not become outcastes if they bring about change in their personal law,. Saudi Arabia and Egypt have not turned into Hindu Raj just because they do not allow cow slaughter. Similarly, Christians have their prayers in regional languages, take Indian names and are imbued with Indian Culture but they still are Christians. If somebody feels the pulls of affection for relatives in Pakistan, it is but natural, but if he celerbrates the defeat of Indian team at the hands of Pakistanis it understandably creates reactions. Even today the Muslims of U.P. and Bihar are leading a refugee life in Pakistan. Hindus and Muslims have always had a relation of give-and-take. Compassion and not pressurization is the need of the hour. Who compelled Rahim, Raskhan, Jayasi and Kare Khan to sing songs of Ram and Krishna? Similarly nobody compels a Hindu to go to the Mazar Chisti in Ajmer Sharif or any other *Aulia*. We still have to discover this culture of compassion fully.

15

POLITICAL SOCIOLOGY OF A MULTI-CULTURAL SOCIETY

JOHN REX

Although a few Right-wing Conservative spokesmen had recently challenged the notion that Britain should be a multi-cultural society and have received some support from intellectuals of the New Right (Honeyford, 1988), the idea that we now do have a multi-cultural society, and that this is not only inevitable but desirable, is widely accepted. Unfortunately it is not at all clear what exactly the term means. Although it purports to being a sociological description, sociologists have done little to clarify the kinds of a structure to which it refers. This paper will, therefore, seek to set out the basis for a political sociology of the multi-cultural society both as an ideal and as a reality, and, while dealing primarily with Britain, indicate what the principle variables are, so laying the basis for a more generally applicable theory.

Multi-cultural and Plural Societies

In the first place the motion of a multi-cultural society has to be distinguished from that of a plural society, on which there is a considerable literature. Furnivall, who first used this concept, used it to refer to a society, such as that which was to be found in colonial Indonesia, in which a number of ethnic encountered each other only in the market-place, and in which, while each of the separate groups was tightly bound together internally by its own morality and culture, this encounter in the market-place was marked by an absence of a "Common will" such as had underpinned market relations in Europe (Furnivall, 1939). M.G. Smith, using Malinowaski's notion of a society as a system of interrelated institutions, argued that in the British West Indies that various ethnic groups which constituted any of these societies each had its own separate and nearly complete institutional set, their incompleteness lying in the fact that they were bound together by a single political system based upon the domination of a ruling group (Smith, 1965). Later Smith was to refer to the *de jure* and *de facto* differential incorporation of the ethnic groups (Smith, 1974). Other writers have sought to apply the theory to African societies in a modified form (Smith and Kuper, 1969) and there has also been a Marxist critique of Smith's and Furnivall's theory which lays emphasis upon the mode and the social relations of production as the element which binds the groups together (Rex, 1986).

What all these theories of the plural society have in common is that they emphasize the inequalities of economic and political power between the society's constituent groups. Thus the South African system, popularly referred to as "apartheid", is seen to be a clear instance of the plural society. Obviously, therefore, when the notion of a multicultural society is discussed as an ideal in the British context, what is being suggested is something sociologically quite different from this, although it may well be the case that the widespread acceptance of the idea of the multi-cultural society has something to do with the fact that some of its supporters envisage a system, in which members of minority groups have unequal rights.

Another type of society from which the multi-cultural society in Britain has to be distinguished is that in which several ethnic groups or nations live together through a system of power-sharing. This does not imply inequality, but the major groups are thought of as maintaining their separate corporate existence while sharing in the exercise of political power. This is the case in Canada where the British and French "founding nations" have shared control of the State, and in Belgium where the Flemish and Walloon populations coexist in terms of a balance of power. It can also be argued that there is power sharing in some colonial societies, such as Malaysia, where one group, the Malay, controls the political system, and another, the Chinese, controls the world of business. Neither of these types of social and political system can be envisaged in Britain and the concept of a multi-cultural society clearly does not imply them.

Cultural Diversity and Equality of Opportunity – The Jenkins Formula

The first official British response to the presence of large numbers of immigrants distinguished by their skin-colour, their language, their religion and their culture was simply to declare that they must be assimilated to a unitary British culture. Thus the Commonwealth Immigrants Advisory Council, referring to educational provision, argued in 1964 that " a national system cannot be expected to perpetuate the different values of immigrant groups" (Commonwealth Immigrants Advisory Council, 1964). This policy was very quickly abandoned, however, and in 1968 the Home Secretary said that what he envisaged was "not a flattering process of uniformity, but cultural diversity, coupled with equal opportunity, in an atmosphere of mutual tolerance" (Patterson, 1958). Since these policy aims have never been formally abandoned, it may be assumed that, in some degree at least, they still influence government policy. In trying to decide what is meant in sociological terms by the concept of a multi-cultural society in the British case, therefore, the Jenkins formula provides us with a starting point.

(a) *Quality of Opportunity and Shared Political Culture of Public Domain*

The most important point to notice about Jenkins' statement is that the notion of cultural diversity is clearly coupled to the distinct notion of equality of opportunity. If, then, it is taken as indicating the British ideal of the multi-cultural society, it is clear that this ideal is not satisfied in any system in which members of the society distinguished by their culture have unequal rights. Presumably, too, the notion of cultural *diversity* does not refer to a situation in which different cultures are thought of as having unequal worth, as is suggested by Honeyford (1988) when he attacks the notion of "cultural relativism".

It is also to be noted, however, that Jenkins speaks only of equality of opportunity and not of equality of outcome or of social rights. Given this minimal commitment, it is not surprising that the formula should have proved acceptable to his conservative successors. More radical, though it is undoubtedly vague, is the ideal informing French policy, the long-established one of "Liberty' Equality and Fraternity"; and, even more radical is the conception of social rights which has enjoyed considerable currency in Britain since the publication of T.H. Marshall's *Citizenship and Social Class* (1950).

Marshall argued that the British working class, having previously won the legal rights of equality before the courts and the political rights which were secured through universal adult suffrage, had, in the Welfare State, now also won a bundle of social rights. For Marshall the range of these new social rights was still quite limited, but, when a Conservative Government succeeded Labour in 1951 and did not reverse its social policies, it was widely thought that there was now a new consensus around certain policies, including planning for full employment, welfare benefits for the sick and the unemployed, free collective bargaining over wages, and the provision of basic social benefits in the form of a free National Health Service, cheap housing for rent and primary and secondary education for all. The radical commitment which such a set of policies involved has, of course, been largely abandoned in the eighties, but it is clear that at times the notion of equal social rights for all citizens in Britain has gone well beyond the limited notion of equality of opportunity enshrined in the Jenkins formula.

The other important point in Marshall's thesis was that, with the achievement of social rights, the primary loyalty of the individual and his or her primary form of belonging, would, in the future, be not to a class, but to the nation. Citizenship rather than class membership was to be the leading concept of Britain's future political sociology. This suggested that, whatever the culture and forms of belonging experienced by individuals as a result of their membership of communal, regional, class, religious and ethnic groups, there was now a shared political culture of the public domain embodied in the idea of citizenship. Such a culture was necessarily unitary and could not be challenged by any concept of multi-culturalism. This is a notion which is implicit in the Jenkins formula when it couples cultural diversity with equality of opportunity.

(b) *Culture Diversity in Private and Communal Domain*

The fact that the Jenkins formula coupled the notion of cultural diversity with equality of opportunity should not, however, be taken to imply that it was not primarily about cultural diversity, but the coupling of these two ideals does involve an inherent difficulty. To insist upon a shared culture of the public domain which emphasizes equality does appear *prima facie* to be at odds with defending the rights of immigrants and ethnic minorities to be different, and it is interesting to notice that in France the emphasis, even in anti-racist organization such as S.O.S. Racisme and France Plus, has been placed on ensuring that members of the ethnic minorities attain the rights of citizenship. Very often this has meant a fear of, or even positive hostility to, immigrant cultures, as when a Black headmaster refused to admit a group of Muslim girls to his school because they were wearing their traditional Muslim scarves.

In Britain what has happened is that recognition has been given to the continuance of minority cultures in the "private" domain of the family and community. Minority groups are thought of as having the right to speak their own languages, to practise their own religions, to have their own domestic and communal culture, and to have their own family arrangements. It has been thought that these forms of diversity can be tolerated and even encouraged since they do not impinge upon the public sphere, and also have a positive value in that they provide social and psychological support for the individual in what otherwise appears as a harsh, individualistic and competitive society. Some would also add that the flourishing of diverse cultures on this level actually "enriches" British culture outside the political and economic sphere.

The doctrine of the two cultural domains was one which was widely shared in discussions of the multi-cultural society, including that by the present author (Rex, 1986b). The notion of equality and citizenship appeared to be saved by declaring it part of the public political domain, while that of cultural diversity was preserved as part of the private communal domain. Those who took this view, therefore, seemed able to get the best of both worlds. Embarrassingly, for them it was also taken up by some of those who did not accept the claims of minority cultures to equal esteem (Honeyford, 1988). For them, however, what the two domains thesis means is that, though the diverse cultures of the minorities may be inferior and even noxious, they may be tolerated so long as the public domain is insulated from them. Moreover, for them, the culture of the public domain is usually represented, not simply as the shared political culture which has been described above, but an all-inclusive British national culture.

Difficulties in the Two Domains Thesis

Having stated the Two Domains Thesis as a starting point for this discussion, it is now necessary to say that it is all naive and simplistic. It involves intellectual difficulties because *prima facie* it appears to be at odds with accepted assumptions in sociological theory and it involves practical difficulties, especially when applied to education, but also in a number of substantive political ways. We should now deal with each of these difficulties in turn.

(a) *Problem of Two Domains Thesis in Sociological Theory*

The mainstream tradition in a sociological theory has always been in some sense functionalist. That is to say, it has argued that the various institutions which constitute a socio-cultural system are all necessarily interrelated so that each helps to sustain the other. Moreover, even the critics of functionalism, who have raised the possibility of inter-institutional or systemic contradictions, have envisaged these very contradictions as leading to a systemic change (Lockwood, 1964), while those who have based their sociology on the notion of class conflict have still analysed the international culture and social organization of the separate classes in functionalist terms (Rex, 1961). There seems to be no place within such sociologies for the idea of two separate socio-cultural domains which have no impact or effect upon one another. The moral values inculcated by the family, for example, are looked at in terms of their functionality or dysfunctionality for performances in the political and economic spheres.

There is, however, also another tradition in sociological and historical thinking. This is that of the secularization thesis. According to this thesis, in the process of modernization, such forms of social organization and culture as the market, bureaucracy and modern technology and science have gradually but systematically been liberated from the controls previously exercised over them by religion, morality and the family. Now, if anything, the liberated institutions come to dominate others, but, at least, they are able to insulate themselves from effect. Herein lies the basis of tolerance. What the secularization thesis does not allow for, however, is the extent to which the modernizing values of the market-place penetrate communal values, or how, on the other hand, the world of the market-place depends upon an individual being socialized within the family and community, and upon their providing a retreat from its rigors (Parsons calls this the Pattern Maintenance and Tension Management System (Parsons,1951).

(b) *Practical Difficulties in the Education System*

Schools in modern societies cannot be simply located in two domains.

On the one hand, they are part of the selective system of an industrial or post-industrial society, submitting their students to competitive testing, and having necessarily to inculcate the values of such a competitive system and of the wider society; on the other, they are concerned with moral education, transmitting the values which are necessary for the individual to become socialized at all, as well as for sustaining communal cultures.

Two kinds of debate go on within the education system. One is about equality of opportunity, with almost all groups demanding that their children should be able to acquire the skills and the qualifications necessary for them to obtain the best occupational positions in their adult lives. Such demands have been made in the past by the working class, despite their former solitary culture induced by the process of class struggle, and they are made equally by immigrant groups, the rationale of whose immigration has been to ensure their children's advancement and increase their earning power. The other is about the preservation of communal values, which are threatened, both by the individualism inherent in the selective process and the economic system, and by the possibility of the host society's communal values being imposed.

Immigrant groups in Britain are almost always committed to the idea of equality of opportunity. Afro-Caribbean parents complain about racism and racist bias in the selective system which prevent their children from obtaining the best results, while Asian parents, even though their children, in most groups, are doing reasonably well, still usually have a highly instrumental attitude to education, and to the possibility that it raises their children's chances of entering the professions or succeeding in business. At the same time racism expresses itself, not simply in unfair selection processes, but also in the denigration of minority values. Afro-Caribbean leaders sometimes attribute the apparently poor performance of their children on this denigration of their culture, while Asians fear that the values which are essential for maintaining the solidarity of their communities will be corrupted by the school.

Investigation of these matters in England was carried out by the Rampton and Swann Committees (Department of Education and Science, 1981, 1985), but inevitably these Committees were given a confused brief. They were required to deal both with the special problem of disadvantage amongst West Indian children and with the problem of potential culture conflict which affected Asian children in particular. Their surprising and somewhat convoluted conclusions were: that the poor performance of some ethnic minority children was due, in the first place, to disadvantages which they shared with poor White working class children, but that they suffered a double disadvantage in that, in addition to sharing these working class disadvantages, they also suffered from racism, both in the wider society and in the schools themselves; that the educational system could amend this situation in part at least by its own practice; and that the way to do this was, on the one hand, to eliminate all elements of racism from the curriculum and from selective processes, and using the disciplinary system to eliminate racist behaviour by teachers and students, and, on the other, to increase respect for minority cultures by introducing all children, including indigenous English children, to them.

Interestingly much of the criticism which has been directed against the Swann Report (see Troyna, 1987; Modgil *et al,* 1987; Verma, 1989; Chivers, 1987) has suggested that it failed to move beyond a multicultural to an anti-racist approach. In fact what this shows is that there was a powerful movement amongst educational theorists and sociologists in favour of greater equality of opportunity, and this movement was certainly right in claiming that the actual proposal was to educate all children in minority cultures. But what is usually less noticed is that the Report had little to say about the value of education in minority cultures of those who adhered to them. This concern was displaced by the radical proposal that all children should be educated in minority as well as majority cultures and thereby equipped to live in an ill-defined multi-cultural society.

In fact the story of the Rampton and Swann Committees is less important than it might have been for the future shape of British society, because its recommendations were not fully acceptable to the Government, and were at best very partially implemented. Actual policies in schools depended far more upon the statements of policy and attempts to implement these statements made by the local education authorities. These statements themselves, however, differ enormously in their proposals and reflect many of the confusions of the Rampton and Swann Committees as well as more besides.

The concern of this paper, however, is not to assess the findings of Rampton and Wann. What concerns us here is the role of the schools in contributing to the creation of a multi-cultural society. On this all that can be said is that the schools were the principal site of the conflicts inherent in the concept of the multi-cultural society itself, and experience shows that it is here above all that the contradictions and difficulties of the Two Domains Thesis become obvious. While it could be argued that the schools could contribute both to sustaining minority cultures as places of socialization and retreat and at the same time offering all children, regardless of race, cultural background, religion or ethnicity, equality of opportunity, this is not what has happened , and parents and children themselves have been left to work out the best balance between the two goals for themselves. Perhaps some Asian families have produced the most viable solution in combining through their own efforts the maintenance of a strong family organization and culture with a very instrumental attitude towards school education and educational success.

The Swann Committee, of course, has, in effect proposed the most radical form of social engineering by suggesting that, as distinct from learning to participate in present majority and minority cultures, all children should acquire a new culture which is an enriched amalgam of all of them. What seems to be the case where this has been tried is that it has simply produced a backlash on the part of majority parents. While it is true that British culture in its non-political aspects is subject to continuous change, it seems unlikely that a new multi-culturally based British culture will be produced by social engineering school.

A final word in this section should be added about Muslim children in schools. More than other groups, the more devout sections of the Muslim community have found difficulty in adapting to the school regime. The absence of provision for religious worship and instruction, the failure of the school meals service to provide *hilal* food, the required exposure of their daughters' bodies in physical education and swimming lessons, and the inaccessibility of single-sex education have all stood in the way of such adaptation. Where these demands have been met, Muslim parents have been prepared, like other immigrant and ethnic minority parents, to regard education instrumentally as a means of material advancement, but some, in any case, have demanded more than this, and have sought through the development of separate schools to prepare their children for living primarily as Muslims, albeit within a secular world.

(c) *Further Substantive Difficulties in the way of Creating a Multi-Cultural Society*

(i) Host Culture, National Culture and Class and Status Cultures: The

ideal of a Multi-Cultural Society spelt out in terms of the Two Domains Thesis sees British society as involving simply a confrontation between private familial and communal cultures, and, in our discussion so far, what we have had in mind in the private sphere have been principally ethnic minority cultures. In such public debate, however, the confrontation is seen as being between "British Culture" in the public domain and the culture of immigrants in the private, and this "British Culture" is not thought of in political terms at all. Rather it is thought of as itself a whole way of life which distinguishes the British from other nations.

National culture in this sense is often bound up with war and international relations as well as with international sport. It is supposed to be a focus of loyalty and patriotism. Those who feel this loyalty most strongly regard immigrant and ethnic minority culture as a threat. This was nicely expressed by the conservative MP, Norman Tebbitt, when, in the course of expressing his doubts about the possibility of a multicultural society, he proposed what he called a "cricket test" asking for whom immigrant groups cheered during cricket matches.

Although this national culture is thought of as involving a host of familiar cultural practices which distinguish the British from, say, the Germans and the French, such familiar practices, and such a way of life are often thought of also in more restricted class terms. British culture tends to be dominated by ways of life developed amongst its upper status groups and fostered in elite schools and universities. These status groups empioy what Parkin (1979), following Weber, calls strategies of "closure", which exclude lower status groups from participation in their way of life. Here the contrast is not with other nations but with other status groups.

Status groups are concerned, as Weber saw, with the differential apportionment of honour (Weber, 1967), but they also come to exercise power. In the British case they exercise considerable control over the Civil Service and over Members of Parliament, and also form alliances with the business classes through which they exercise economic power. While the business classes seek legitimation of their own position through marital alliances and through sending their children to elite schools, the upper classes become members of Boards of Directors.

As against these strategies of closure and class alliance, other status groups develop their own district cultures. T.S. Eliot, in his *Notes Towards a Definition of Culture,* (1945) which was primarily a defence of upper class culture, noted that the working classes developed cultures of their own, often of a regional sort; Raymond Williams in his *Culture and Society* (1953) spoke of a "Common Culture" distinct from the restricted culture of ruling groups; and Richard Hoggart, in his *Uses of Literacy* (1957), gave an evocative account of the cultural and moral values of working class culture in Hunslet in Leeds.

Just as the culture of upper-status group becomes interwined with the class culture of the business classes, however, so this popular culture becomes interwined with the culture of the working classes, understood in a more political sense. A working class culture emerges in the course of defensive and offensive class struggles based upon strong themes of solidarity, and this is projected into a national stage through the Labour Party. Such a culture disputes the claim of the culture of upper-status groups and classes to being a national culture.

Finally, one should note the importance of the culture of the middle classes. Members of these classes often reject the solidarity of working class culture and emphasize individualism and self-help, without becoming incorporated into the closed culture of upper-status groups and classes.

What one has in Britain, therefore, is not a unitary British culture, but rather a hierarchy of cultures, which, to some extent, constitute cultural strata, but which are also based upon the political fact of class struggle. This is the culture which immigrant and ethnic minority cultures confront.

(b) *The Disputed Political Culture of the Public Domain*

Earlier we spoke of a shared culture of the public domain. What we can now see is that there is a considerable degree of dispute within this culture. The upper-status groups use strategies of closure; the business classes seek entry into the world of their status superiors; the working classes emphasize the virtue of solidarity and equality; and the middle classes emphasize equality of opportunity.

The shared political culture of the public domain arises out of the compromises which are made between these various tendencies. It is based upon the notion of hard-own rights centring on the notions of equality of opportunity and equality of outcome. Political parties are bound to make some reference to these ideals. However much upper-class conservatives may wish to defend their closed class culture and their class rule, the Conservative Party is bound to subscribe to the ideal of equality of opportunity, or even, recently, to the idea of a classless society. Labour on the other hand, emphasizes equality of outcome. Sometimes one ideal gains the ascendancy, sometimes the other, but over the longer term what emerges is a new compromise based upon the idea of a minimum which is equally available to all, coupled with superior rewards for some, conceived of as a reward for effort.

The relationship of immigrant and ethnic minority cultures to this system is necessarily complex. On the one hand, they find their own cultures placed within a hierarchy of cultures, and their individual members having to face, not only the strategies of closure of the upper classes, but also those based upon what Parkin (1979) calls the strategies of usurpatory culture of the working classes. On the other, their members must make what claims they can within whatever is the going system of rights available in the public domain. They may seek to preserve their own solidary cultures while seeking in an instrumental way to benefit from equal opportunity policies, or they may come to share some of the values of the working classes, the middle classes or the business classes.

Race relations legislation in Britain complicates these problems. It is primarily designed to secure equality of opportunity for members of ethnic minority groups, but it also sometimes seems to be aiming at equality of outcome imposed by what Honeyford (1988) calls a regulatory bureaucracy. Inevitably, therefore, it produces resentment, both among the middle classes whose ideal is simply equality of opportunity, and amongst the working classes whose rights have been won, not through the interventions of a benevolent government, but, much more, through hard political struggle. Thus, however much ethnic minority groups might seek participation in the shared political culture of the public domain, they find themselves faced with additional suspicions and hostility.

(c) *Religion in the Public Domain*

Another questionable assumption in the ideal model of a multi-cultural society, which we have outlined, is that Britain is a secular State, and that religion is a private matter. There is some truth in this in that it is in no sense a theocracy, and that a variety of forms of religious belief and practice are tolerated, but the notions of a secular State and secular State education are not nearly as clearly defined as they are, for instance, in France.

In fact the Anglican Church in Britain has a privileged position and even some symbolic power. The Archbishop of Canterbury actually crowns the Monarch, and the Church endorses State institutions on many public occasions, especially those connected with war. Not surprisingly the Archbishop was criticized by the Prime Minister for having failed to strike a sufficient note of triumph in his sermon at a memorial service after the successful completion of the Falklands war.

The various churches also provide supernatural recognition of individual life events, such as birth, marriage and death, and their religious functionaries provide a counselling service for many people at times of individual and family crises; the schools provide occasions for Christian religious worship and instruction; and Church spokesmen are expected to make statements on social and political matters such as the plight of the homeless or of inner city people generally, even though these are expected to avoid any kind of party political commitment (see, for example, *Faith in the City,* the report of Archbishop's Committee on Urban Priority Areas (ACUPA, 1985).

None of this, of course, adds up to more than the exercise of symbolic power by the churches, and in return for this symbolic power, they are kept firmly in their place. Although the Monarch is crowned by the Archbishop he/she is also known as the Supreme Governor of his church; the church is expected to support the interests of the nation in wartime; and, where it does make apparently political interventions, these are expected to be of a general moral kind rather than being precise political directives to legislators in Parliament.

Nonetheless the special role of the Christian church, and the Anglican church in particular, does have some significance for any attempt to create a multi-cultural society. They appear to endorse a national and nationalist culture rather than a society based upon a plurality of cultures; they have a privileged position in the schools, and they even have the protection of a law against blasphemy, which is at odds with the general commitment of the political culture of the public domain to freedom of speech.

From the point of view of immigrant and ethnic minorities this privileged position of Christianity does make their integration into British society more difficult. Though they have formally established their right to opt out of religious worship in schools and to have worship of their own, they have in fact to struggle and argue to enforce this right, and, on the major question of protecting their religions against blasphemy, they have been sharply reminded, since the publication of Rushdie's *The Satanic Verses* (1988) that their religions do not enjoy the protection accorded to Christianity. As some of their more devout members see it, they are cultural and religious aliens in a Christian society, while, from the point of view of cultural equality, they face a national culture with a religious endorsement which is not available to minority cultures.

(d) *Human Rights and Minority Cultures*

In Britain, in common with other advanced industrial societies, discourse within the public domain does not usually stop at the discussion of equality of opportunity or of equal social right in the Marshallian sense. It also extends to the question of individual human rights and it is here that it brings the very foundations of ethnic minority social organization and culture into question. This is particularly true of the discourse of feminism. To many feminists the position of women in the minority cultures appears unacceptable, and they see themselves as having a concern for the liberation of wives and daughters from the domination of their menfolk. Though ethnic minority spokesmen may claim that they are concerned to protect their womenfolk from the corruption of a secular capitalist society, and that their forms of arranged marriage and extended kinship are essential strengths in their community organization, they are likely to find their cultures continually under attack from these quarters. There is a certain irony in this, in that feminists often see their campaigns on questions of gender equality as paralleling campaigns for the equality of ethnic minorities.

(e) *Demands by Ethnic Minorities in the Public Domain*

The model of the Multi-Cultural Society based upon the Two Domains does not, however, encounter only those difficulties which arise from the British side. For some minority groups and minority religions, and, particularly, Islam, the division between public and private domains appears unacceptable. For most Muslims, Islam is not merely a private matter but a whole way of life. Some, though by no means all, Muslims believe in the idea of an Islamic State; there is widespread expectation that the State should protect religion; Islam has its own economic ethics, which are in some ways at odds with capitalism, it has its own ideas about education; and, not least, as we have seen in the previous section, its own view on the position of women and the family.

In fact Islam has a long history and Muslims have in the past found ways of living in non-Muslim and secular societies. They do not necessarily all share the belief, to be found in the teachings like those of Maududi, the founder of Jamaat-i-Islami, in the ideal of an Islamic State; they have found ways of pursuing their banking and business in capitalist societies; they have found way of adjusting to predominantly secular education; and, even on the question of the rights of women, their discourse is by no means as reactionary and patriarchal as many Western feminists assume. It is misleading, therefore, to suggest that anyone who practises Islam is a so-called "fundamentalist" whose irrationality makes it impossible for him to live in a multi-cultural society.

To say this, however, is by no means to say that there are no difficulties in the way of finding a place for Islam in British society. In the immediate future it may well be that some extreme Muslims may make demands which appear unacceptable to most British people, as is evident from the recent publication of *The Muslim Manifesto* (Muslim Institute, 1990) by a relatively small and unrepresentative body called The Muslim Institute, which calls for the establishment of a Muslim Assembly, and a speech by the Institute's leader, Kalim Siddiqui (Siddiqui, 1990) calling for a special relationship between British Muslims and the State of Iran. On the other hand the tendency to dismiss all Islam as "fundamentalist" may make it impossible even for the more moderate to be accepted as legitimate citizens. In the immediate future, then considerable religious and ethnic conflict seems likely, even, though, in the longer run dialogue and negotiation might lead to the discovery that Muslim and Christian/British notions of the public domain are not incompatible.

Other ethnic and religious minorities have found it easier to come to terms with living in Britain than have Muslims. It still has to be noted, however, that, even though they might adapt very readily to living in Britain and taking the economic opportunities which living there offers, many of them may remain oriented in their thinking to homeland politics. Sikhs may use their British base to campaign for a separate State of Khalistan, Mirpuris may campaign for what they see as the liberation of Kashmir, and many West Indians, finding themselves rejected in what appears to them to be a racist Britain, may hunger for an African Zion. A multi-cultural Britain, may well have to recognize that the continuance of such commitments is part of the culture of the private domain which can be tolerated, even though it prevents some ethnic minority members from becoming completely and finally British.

Possible Outcomes

The aim of this paper has not been one of simple advocacy. What it does, having outlined an ideal model, is to consider some of the difficulties which stand in the way of its realization. It is an exercise in political sociology, and the task of the sociologist is not simply to provide happy endings. All that he can do is to suggest possible outcomes, leaving it to activists to pursue this or that political ideal, including that of the Multi-Cultural Society. It is to the task of considering realistically what these outcomes may be that we must now, finally, turn.

One important possibility which should not be neglected is that over several generations present problems and difficulties may grow less acute. Many of the descendants of immigrants may become less concerned with the perpetuation of their own cultures and more concerned with economic success in Britain. They may also find themselves affiliating to the class cultures and organizations of their indigenous peers. It would be "optimistic" to believe that this process will occur as easily and smoothly as it has over two or three generations amongst European immigrants in America, because, at least so far as British Asian immigrants are concerned, they have great cultural and organizational strengths, based on cultures and religions in their homelands, more different from those indigenous to Britain than were the cultures of America's European immigrants from those of the United States. Nonetheless this does not mean that there will be no process of adaptation and acculturation.

The second more immediate and likely possibility is the continuance of conflict on all the levels we have discussed. Conflict will go on about the place of multi-culturalism in education; British nationalism and racism are likely to continue in ways which deny ethnic minority cultures recognition and individual members of these minorities equality of opportunity; outcome for ethnic minority members will continue to provoke a backlash in the indigenous community; many members of the indigenous working class will continue to pursue strategies of usurpationary closure against the minorities, particularly if economic circumstances are such that their own livelihood seems threatened; ethnic minority cultures may continue to be attacked by human rights activists; and, finally, minority cultures may be slow to adapt to living in a secular multi-cultural society, the more so if their adherents feel that they are not fully members of that society.

If, however, societies attempting to be multi-cultural are likely to be societies in conflict for the foreseeable future, it should not be thought that this necessarily means everlasting riots and street demonstrations, even though there may be substantial and violent disturbances. Just as, in earlier times, class conflicts which started in circumstances of riot and disorder gave way to processes of negotiation and compromise, so the relationship of ethnic minorities to British society will be renegotiated. This will include not merely a redefinition of the extent to which differences in the private and communal spheres are tolerated or encouraged, but also a renegotiation of the political culture of the public domain. So far as this latter is concerned, what may occur is that when minority aims are understood, it may well emerge that the political ideals of the minority, as well as their ideas about human rights, are not so different from those of the majority, Muslims, for example, being very supportive, for their own religious reasons, of the idea of the Welfare State. On the other hand, British class-based cultures may be seen as matters of private preference rather than as demanding some sort of overall hegemony, while the privileged role of Christian religion might also come to be questioned in a secular State.

To recognize this third possibility does not, however, involve pointing, after all, to an inevitable happy ending. What it should do is to record the fact that, in a society which has to deal with cultural diversity, while there may be continuing conflicts, there may also be dialogue, and, arising out of such dialogue, negotiations and compromise. The actuality as opposed to the ideal of the Multi-Cultural Society will, in fact, be found in a continuing process of both conflict and compromise.

Post-Script

The Relevance of this Argument for Other Societies

What I have written is based upon an analysis of the British case. It looks at the political and sociological factors in Britain which make it difficult to realize the ideal of multi-cultural society understood as one which combines the notion of equal opportunity for all with that of cultural diversity and mutual tolerance. The variables involved here, however, are relevant to other societies. In all cases one has to ask the following questions:

1. How far is there a shared political culture in the public domain based upon the notion of equal opportunity?
2. To what extent is this shared political culture, if it does exist, subordinated to a nationalist culture of a dominant ethnic group, or an upper-class or caste culture?
3. To what extent is there a secular State and to what extent does the State represent a particular religion and draw for its legitimacy on that religion?
4. To what extent is there a recognition of a private communal domain in which differences of language, religion and culture are tolerated?
5. To what extent are minority cultures and religions able to accept the idea of a secular State and their own confinement to the private and communal sphere?

The Indian Case

It would be absurd for a visitor to India to make major judgements of a political kind about the structure of Indian society. Given the above theoretical framework and the questions to which it leads, however, the following would appear to be the issues posed for Indian political sociologists:

1. Clearly, Parliamentary Democracy and a Secular Political Order have survived in India to a degree unparalleled in the post-imperial world. How far is this form of government and political order secure? It is likely to be subverted by the domination of the society by groups based on class, caste or communal religions which seek to impose their dominance in the public sphere?
2. How far is a political culture based upon equality of opportunity achievable and sustainable in a society in which caste remaining an important factor?
3. How far are the various religious groups willing to accept a *modus vivendi* based upon mutual tolerance? Does the claim of

politicized Hinduism that India should be a Hindu country, of the belief of some Muslims in the ideal of an Islamic State, make such a *modus vivendi* impossible, or are there sufficient numbers amongst those practising the various religions as well as among secular politicians whose pragmatic rather than dogmatic beliefs make mutual cooperation in a single society possible?

4. In so far as those who practise the various religions are unable to accept the idea of a purely secular State, is it nonetheless possible for them through dialogue to arrive at a set of shared political values on which the State and the political order might be based?
5. These questions were raised prior to the elections of May 1991, but it may well be that they will be as relevant after the elections as they were for Premier V.P. Singh in 1990.

BIBLIOGRAPHY

1. ACUPA (1985), *Faith in the City —Report of the Archbishop's Committee on Urban Priority Areas,* Church House, London.
2. Chievers, T. (1987), *Race and Culture in Education,* National Foundation for Educational Research/Nelson, London.
3. Commonwealth Immigrants Advisory Council (1964), Third Report, Cmnd 2458, N.M.S.O., London.
4. Department of Education and Science (1981), *Report of the Committee of Enquiry into the Education of Children from Minority Groups —Interim Report: West Indian Children in our Schools.* (Chairman Mr. Anthony Rampton), Cmnd 8273, H.M.S.O., London.
5. Department of Education and Science (1985), *Education for All: Report of the Committee of Enquiry into the Education of Children from Minority Groups,* Vol. II (Chairman Lord Swann), Cmnd 9453, H.M.S.O., London.
6. Eliot, T.S. (1948), *Notes Towards a Definition of Culture,* Faber, London.
7. Furnivall, J.S. (1939), *Netherland India —A Study of Plural Economy,* Cambridge University Press, Cambridge.
8. Hoggart, R. (1957), *The Uses of Literacy,* Chatto and Windus, London.
9. Honyford, R. (1988), *Integration or Disintegration,* Claridge Press, London.
10. Lockwood, D. (1964), "Social Integration and System Integration" in Zollschan, G.K. and Hirsch, M. (eds), *Explorations in Social Change,* Houghton Mifflin, Boston.
11. Marshall, T.H. (1950), *Citizenship and Social Class,* Cambridge University, Cambridge.
12. Modgil, S., Verma, G., Mallick, K., and Modgil, C. (1957), *Multi-cultural Education — The Interminable Debate,* Falmer, Brighton.
13. Muslim Institute (1990), *The Muslim Manifesto,* Muslim Institute, London.

14. Parsons, T., (1951), *The Social System*, Routledge and Kegan Paul, London.

15. Patterson, S. (1968), *Immigrants in Industry*, Oxford University Press for the Institute of Race Relations, London.

16. Rex, J. (1961), *Key Problems of Sociological Theory*, Routledge and Kegan Paul, London.

17. Rex, J. (1986a), *Race and Ethnicity*, Open University Press, Milton Keymes.

18 Rex, J. (1986a), *The Concept of a Multi-cultural Society*, Centre for Research in Ethnic Relations, University of Wàrwick, Coventry.

19. Rushdie, S. (1988), *The Satanic Verses*, Vikas Books, London.

20. Siddiqui Kalim (1990), "Generating Power without Politics"' Unpublished Address to a Conference of the Muslim Institute, London.

21 Smith, M.G. (1965), *The Plural Society in the British West Indies*, University of California Press, Berkeley.

22. Smith, M.G. (1974), *Corporations and Society*, Duckworth, London.

23. Smith, M.G. and Kuper, L. (Eds) (1969), *Pluralism in Africa*, University of California Press, Berkeley.

24. Troyna, B. (1987), (Ed), *Racial Inequality in Education*, Tavistock, London.

25. Verma, G. (Ed) (1989), *Education for All — A Landmark in Pluralism*, Falmer, Brighton.

26. Weber, M. (1967), *Economy and Society*, Bedminter Press, New York.

27. Williams, R. (1963), *Culture and Society*, Pelican Books, Harmondsworth.

16

CONCLUSION

ALI ASHRAF

That there is often tension between ethnic identity and national or regional integration is undeniable. Identity of an individual or group and their integration with a larger entity are opposite tendencies that assert to express themselves in diverse and often contradictory directions. The Hegelian dialectics works towards both antithesis and synthesis, and Hegel might well be right but for the fact that the process does not seem to end with the establishment of nation-states. We do not witness the end of history even with the establishment of American supremacy at this time. History seems to rule out a final and static resolution of conflicts, and the process of antagonism and reconciliation goes on. The only salutary strategy would be to make the process productive of a harmonious reconciliation through peaceful resolution of conflicts. The contemporary world is passing through a process of rapid and far-reaching changes, most conspicuously with the collapse of the Soviet Union, and a trend towards regional integration in Europe. An urge for larger than national integration and a reaction against totalitarian unity offer lessons for other experiments in self-determination through autonomy and integration.

Cultural Identity

A people sharing the same language and culture and the consciousness of a common group entity needs autonomy for the cultivation and improvement of its identity. An individual or group seeks to avoid alienation and attain moral development through the roots where these are well embedded in the social structure, language and literature, and a communication network. The preservation of "Community" feeling is vital. The question arises as to how a community relates to other communities and the larger entity of Nation, State or Region, and the world at large.

One is confronted with the fact that in modern times there is hardly a State, howsoever small, that is completely homogeneous in race, religion, language and culture. Conquests, annexations, mobility and migrations, culture and commerce have encouraged peoples of different stocks, languages and religions to cross the borders and make for social and cultural heterogeneity. History also shows how the maps of countries have been changing: wars, peace settlements, liberation movements, regional arrangements or voluntary associations contribute to the changes in State boundaries.

The upshot is that most States in modern times tend to be multi-ethnic entities. How this multiplicity of races, religions and languages are tackled in different sets of political arrangements is an illuminating exercise. A look at the phenomenon of ethnicity and integration in the USA, the USSR and India would throw some light on different patterns of relationship between ethnic identity and political integration. The USA is a nation of migrants, initially from European countries and recently from all over the world. Such diversity of backgrounds would make it very difficult to achieve any measure of viable unity, but the dominance of WASP (White Anglo-Saxon Protestant) as a cultural and political "Centre" and the constitutional framework of Democracy and Federation with effective political institutions have fostered political integration and public order on the basis of cultural assimilation.

The Soviet Union followed the pattern of expansion on a vast territory including those regions inhabited by different ethnic communities of Central Asia and East Europe as well as the Baltic States. Communism and the constitutional right to secede notwithstanding, the non-Russian Republics could be kept within the Soviet Union through the process of totalitarian regimentation by the party, the bureaucracy and the military. The process of democratization and restructuring has loosened the Soviet Union which has become untendable with the unilateral declaration of independence by most of the Republics. The multi-ethnic State of the Soviet Union has broken up with a number of States seceding from it and the rest forming a nominal Commonwealth of Independent States.

Of the two models mentioned above the American model is based on assimilation where the Anglo-Saxon culture has prevailed and absorbed the migrant minorities in the mainstream of a monolithic culture. The ethnic character of minorities is preserved only in name, in food, festivals, music and memories. But the juggernaut of modernization, media and mass society creates force for homogenization and facilitates assimilation of ethnic diversity. De Toqueville perceived the dangers and pitfalls of a mass society in the American democracy of the 19th century. The danger has multiplied in this century on account of technological, economic and social change and the electronic media, and is a source of alienation for ethnic minorities. The national unity is, however, secure in the supremacy of the political elite and mass culture.

The Russian model has suffered essentially from lack of democratic freedom and economic success. The economic inefficiency and imbalances of the Soviet system have fanned the fires of ethnicity; and the liberalization process has weakened the will and provides full scope for ethnic assertions amounting to secession.

As against these, the Indian model has nourished its diversity and from the beginning of national movement recognized diversity of language, culture and religion as an organic character of Indian civilization, society and polity. The Hindu culture allowed diversity to flourish within the framework of a hierarchical society. Mahatma Gandhi was a constructive and creative force in this sphere. It is not the place to repeat the teachings of Gandhiji, but it is necessary to emphasize that Truth for him was essentially non-alienation, and attachment to one's language, culture and religion was vital and also consistent with one's concern for humanity. Swadeshi was the method by which one could realize the ideals of ethical individualism and personal integrity, the basic tenet of his world outlook. Mahatma Gandhi's deep faith in religion precluded neither secularism nor humanism. He believed that "if religion dies then India dies". However, he also maintained that "Today Hindus and Muslims are clinging to the husk of religion." His deep faith in spiritual values did not preclude the changes in scriptures and practices if these were against the status and honour of women or "untouchables", for example. The following observations of Gandhiji are quite relevant to the issue of ethnic identity and national integration:

> "India cannot cease to be one nation because people belonging to different religions live in it.........
>
> "Linguistic redistribution should not militate against the organic unity of India.

"In the India for whose fashioning I have worked all my life, everyone enjoys equality of status, whatever his religion is. The state is bound to be wholly secular.

"Religion is no test of nationality, but a personal matter between man and his God." ("The Message of Mahatma Gandhi" by Mohan Rao in *India is One Nation*, pp. 69, 70, 73.)

Secularism and Minorityism

Ethnicity has often been the problem of minorities in that they seek protection from the action or influence of the majority. The ethnic groups claim rights on account of their minority status: the French Canadians, the American Jews, blacks or Catholics, the Muslims or blacks in France, South Asians in the U.K., Turks in Germany; Central Asians in the USSR, Tamils in Sri Lanka, and the religious or linguistic minorities in India, Pakistan or Bangladesh. In India, however, there has been in recent years an upsurge in some parties and organizations of the majority community to demand assertion of their identity and power. This is a trend that may be traced to the movement of *Hindutva* in 1923, but in its volume and velocity it is a new force. The complaint of the contemporary protagonists of *Hindutva* is that minorities in general and the Muslims in particular have been taking advantage of the political parties that follow a policy of appeasement towards the Muslims. It is alleged that minorities want to enjoy a privileged position on the following issues/grounds:

1. Separate Personal Laws:
2. Special status of minority languages,
3. Minority character of educational institutions,
4. Use of vote banks for political support,
5. The Minorities Commission.

The criticism of what is called minorityism is directed against government policies of accommodation towards the demands and pressures of minorities. The tendency of the Government to acquiesce into the pressures of orthodox elements for opportunistic electoral reasons illustrates the point. On the other hand, there is no evidence that the Hindu majority is a captive in the hands of minorities. In fact democracy as it is practised in the world is always a bargaining system and special interests exert their influence in their favour. The concessions made to linguistic or regional or caste groups are more numerous and momentous in their consequences than those made to minorities in India. The history of the linguistic reorganization of States, the concessions to regional autonomy in the matter of language and education, the provisions of reservations for the depressed castes are all much more important for the State than anything done for the minorities in general.

The phenomenon of minorityism is bound up with the politics of democracy, of elections and the vote banks. The issue tends to be acrimonious during the erosion of political institutions and the weakening of public authority and order. The *Hindutva* strategy, on the other hand, is aimed at the imposition of national unity on a monolithic basis. Its aim is not only to ensure that the concern for the ethnic identity does not violate and damage the cause of national unity, but to establish it on the basis of Hindu Rashtra, exclusive Hindu culture and traditions, and the one common civil code and uniform institutions and laws in utter disregard of different domains of public and private life, and without conceding any sign of different, much less separate, identity for the minority groups.

Dynamics of Ethnicity and Nationalism

Multi-ethnic, multi-national States are unavoidable especially in the context of the Third World. In modern times, States cannot be built on national or ethnic homogeneity. Neither exchange of population nor modernization can ensure complete correspondence between Ethnicity and State. To draw the map of the world on this basis would be impossible and any attempt even in a region could create chaos, and incalculable hardship, much more than was witnessed in the mid-forties in this subcontinent. Moreover, given the diversity of races, religions and languages, the logical conclusion of making States on the basis of ethnic homogeneity would destroy the viability of such States as economic and strategic entities.

The discussion at some length of the minority question without reference to the fissiparous tendencies in India and especially in the secessionist demands in some regions as also the inter-State squabbles over land and water disputes may appear somewhat lopsided and calculated to sideline the issues of Kashmir, Punjab, Tamil Nadu, Assam or North-Eastern region as a whole. Our conclusion, however, is that the problem of identity and integration in India has been too much confined to the need for assimilation of ethnic minorities in the mainstream of nationalism.

The trend in the last decade has been towards highlighting the minority religions as the major obstacle to national integration. Blame is too often put on the religious aspirations and demands of the Muslims, Christians and Sikhs, in respect of both their *cultural* problems as a minority wherever in India they may be and their *regional* aspirations in Kashmir, North-East and Punjab. It is important to consider the cultural and regional problems separately. The demand for autonomy in Kashmir, Punjab and North-East is regional and ethnic. The special provisions for safeguarding of property rights as well as ethnic culture is a special feature of the regional ethnic minorities. This is a problem linked with *constitutional* relationship between the Central Government and the State Governments. This is primarily a problem of evolving a *federal* form of government that can ensure full autonomy to States in so far as the management of a State is concerned; it also involves questions of regional imbalances and the allocation of Central resources for the development of backward or remote regions. The issue of Centre-State relationship has bedevilled the Indian polity since independence and is not confined to the ethnic minorities. The conflicts between the Centre and States have been equally serious in practically all the states on the ground of Central interference with and intervention in the affairs of the State Governments. It may as well be argued that the aggravation or exacerbation of relations with Kashmir, Punjab or Assam is due to wrong and short-sighted policies of the Central Government itself. Indeed it can be argued that the demand of autonomy has been directly related to the ruling parties at the Centre.

The problem regarding cultural identity and integration of linguistic and religious minorities on the other hand is a matter of State Government policies pertaining to education and employment and opportunities for religious and educational rights. The problem has often arisen because of the dichotomy between the declarations of democratic pluralism and minority rights on the one hand and the actual policies denying the minorities an adequate safeguard of their cultural and educational rights in the field of religion and language on the other. The neglect of Urdu highlights the prejudice of the majority against the language of a minority, which feels that if this is the plight of Urdu, a language of Hindu-Muslim unity and an emblem of composite culture, what else is safe from the blight of communal hostility. The provision for the teaching of Urdu is woefully inadequate, and the

Centre's policy of three-language formula in school education is observed mostly in its breach. The hostility to Urdu is difficult to understand when the Muslims have accepted Hindi as a compulsory subject and as the medium of instruction. Urdu is also a language which is popular in the market-place and in ordinary conversations, and its literature presents a humanist and secular worldview which is in refreshing contrast to the orthodoxy of the theological literature. Urdu as such could offer a foil to the theological culture of the clergy and could be a bond of positive relationship between the Muslims and non-Muslims. The Muslim institutions of education and training are known to suffer from many discriminatory practices of the State administration which are often contrary to the policies of the Centre.

The fact of the matter is that the explosion of movements and organizations like the Shiv Sena, Bajrang Dal, Vishwa Hindu Parishad and the Bhartiya Janata Party and their demand for national unity on the basis of one uniform religious and cultural pattern poses a major threat to the cause of national integration as well as religious and linguistic identity of various groups. No one can doubt the dedication and concern of Gandhiji with Hinduism and yet he declined to make it the basis of Indian polity. The supreme achievement of the Mahatma was to emphasize the value of religion and language as the matrix of one's cultural tradition and at the same time to attempt to reform this tradition to fit in with the value of equality and justice. The Mahatma instilled a sense of pride among the Indians in their respective traditions and in the common framework of a pluralistic culture and polity. The current movement of *Hindutva*, based on deep prejudice and hatred for the Muslims is a repudiation of every tenet of Gandhiji; and is in complete contrast to the Mahatma's absolute commitment to non-violence, and respect for identity and integrity of all. An underlying danger is that while minority communalism has been a problem in free India's administration of law and order, the *Hindutva* threatens to alter the nature of Indian polity, society and culture.

The question of regional and cultural identity and integration in India is closely linked with the issue of good government and self-government. The erosion of government authority, the rise of criminality and corruption and the failure of the political process to respond effectively to the problems of governance has cost India the respect of all concerned. The "soft" State in its ultimate degeneration is a matter of ridicule, and it is not only a matter of ridicule, but also the cause of concern over the rise of forces that seek to upset the balance between ethnic identity and political integration of the subcontinent as a whole. The world is at the threshold of change; and regional entities are trying to emerge to cope with the problems of economic development, safeguard the environment and maintenance of peace through cooperation. If such a vision is valid for South Asia also, the platform of *Hindutva* is an impediment to an evolution of a South Asian community as well as Indian democracy in an effective form. The root of the problem is the lack of a dynamic, resilient and constructive political force, which is unencumbered by irrational and negative hang-ups of the past and is prepared to march towards the goals of freedom and civility, truth and justice for all, and to march without hatred and fear, and without resort of violence, to a common destiny in an integrative framework of understanding and cooperation.

It is important to note the imperatives of contemporary trends towards multi-national regional associations. The European Community as well as other organizations of regional cooperation are pointers towards the future. The right of self-determination with which the present century began and which became a political creed of liberalism was indeed a movement against despotic empires. The attempts at regional cooperation is a response to the economic and technological demands of our times which was accompanied with the realization that peace and cooperation among nation-states is a necessary condition for social, economic and ecological improvements. A new World Order is still a remote dream. However the goals of peace and prosperity as also those of economic and ecological balance can be achieved through organizations of regional cooperation. The example of European Community is worth emulation. South Asia, or West Asia, South East Asia and other distinct regions have no constructive alternative but to pursue political development of democracy, decentralisation, autonomy and cooperation on a regional basis to prevent disorder and discord among nations. In so far as South Asia is concerned, geography and economy, history and culture provide plenty of basis for both cultural autonomy and secular integration, provided concern for identity is not so narrowly interpreted as to preclude necessary reforms in laws and institutions governing the secular spheres of life.

Various perspectives and suggestions emerge out of the viewpoints presented in the Seminar. These may be summarized as follows:

It is necessary to reject the conventional, Western concept of a nation-state that consists of homogeneous and cohesive community of people united by one national identity, sustained by the dominance of a common centre of culture and politics. This would not suit the conditions of socio-cultural and ethnic diversity and pluralism prevailing in India, and for that matter, in most of the Third World countries. On the other hand it is equally necessary to reject the assertion of divisive forces for ethnic self-determination outside the common framework of a constitutional and political framework in order to avoid dismemberment of State and political instability resulting from a threat of secession and civil wars.

What is imperative, therefore, is to maintain a framework of democratic and federal centre with provision for adequate autonomy and decentralisation to allow the ethnic minorities with opportunities of participation in the regional and national civic and political life. This centre need not be one dominant culture directing politics in accordance with the interests of one religious group, but should be a cultural and political framework that is pluralist and accommodative. The concept of the Framework rather than a Centre is a unique and signal contribution of India to the political development of multi-ethnic societies.

It is often suggested that modernization or socio-economic change and an industrial civilization would help remove differences and disparities as among various ethnic and social groups and help promote national unity. Economic well-being and social mobility do help in removing social tensions and encourage understanding and tolerance. It is, however, doubtful that modernization *per se* succeeds in obliterating the cultural identities of the ethnic groups or regional communities. Also under Indian conditions where religious and cultural identities are valued and nourished along with secular identities of nationalism or caste, it is all the more problematic whether modernization will create a homogeneity of cultural, ethnic or even social identity. It is, therefore, a safe assumption that divergence of language and culture and religion will survive social and economic development.

The realistic solutions to the problem of a healthy and viable relationship between ethnic identity and national unity, therefore, would require political measures and mechanisms to allow and encourage political and civic participation among the social groups, to evolve a broad national consensus on the common framework and rules of the game to determine the scope and competence of the central authority *vis-a-vis* several constituent authorities; and to provide for 'Two domains' of political culture so as to permit a private domain of group identities and special laws and institutions of family, marriage and inheritance along with the public domain of secular interests like public services, and administrative infrastructure with competence and responsibility for the health and well-being of the nation as well as individual citizens regardless of ethnic, cultural or religious identity.

These political solutions must be directed towards (i) federal divisions of powers between the Centre and States and further devolution of power for the district and local authorities and (ii) democratic pluralism so as to allow not only competition but also autonomy for the management of educational and cultural affairs on a municipal/local as well as State levels.

As Prof. Sachchidananda rightly observed: There can be no integration without participation and a share in the political as well as cultural life of the country. On the other hand, participation must be fostered and sustained by the practice of fairness and justice to inspire confidence in and identification with the larger national concerns and interests. Elections are a common democratic means of ensuring participation of citizens in the choice of their representatives. The subversion of the electoral process so that elections have ceased to be free and fair in India has undermined the value and credibility of elections as a means of political participation. The point, therefore, bears repetition that political parties must strive to establish credibility and legitimacy through a genuine practice of political accountability, and of social justice and fair play before they can expect to get political support for themselves and for public interest. Differences and conflicts of interests are what make a democratic polity. To lament diversity of social or ethnic interest is no way to build a polity of democracy. To find in the concern for ethnic identity a challenge or obstacle to national integration is to indulge in the politics of scapegoats. What we need is authentic, mature and effective politics to build on our assets which, fortunately and in spite of apparent difficulties, are many. It is the asset of a long and mature and stable civilization, and of an imperishable cushion to absorb the shocks and vicissitudes of history that inspires faith and hope for the future of India even in the midst of its perils and problems. The urgent task is to convert the cultural asset into the political energy and intellectual vision to maintain and improve India's proverbial unity in diversity within a viable, free and just polity.

INDEX